A HISTORY LOVER'S GUIDE TO CHEYENNE

A History Lover's Guide to
CHEYENNE

Starley Talbott and Michael E. Kassel

The History PRESS

Published by The History Press
Charleston, SC
www.historypress.com

Front cover, top left: The Tivoli Building, 1880s, at the corner of Carey Avenue and 16th Street. *Photograph by Michael Dixon*; *middle*: A north side view of the Wyoming State Capitol shows the brilliant chandelier in the window of the restored Territorial House Chamber. *Photograph by Starley Talbott*; *right*: A cowboy demonstrates riding skills at the world's largest outdoor rodeo. *Photograph by Christine Kronz*.
Front cover, bottom: The grand Romanesque-style Union Pacific Railroad Depot was designated a National Historic Landmark in 2006. *Photograph by Michael Dixon*.
Back cover, top: A Union Pacific "Big Boy" steam engine is on display at Holliday Park. *Photograph by Michael Dixon*; *bottom*: The Nagle-Warren Mansion, built in 1888, on 17th Street. *Photograph by Michael Dixon*.

First published 2021

Manufactured in the United States

ISBN 9781467149525

Library of Congress Control Number: 2021943428

CONTENTS

FOREWORD

The history of the city of Cheyenne can be told through its buildings and monuments. The structures speak from the past, giving a solid framework for the future. Cheyenne's history of railroads, aviation and people has had major impacts on the growth of our nation, not just the state of Wyoming. Buildings are the most visible evidence of the past. They create the ambiance for the city of Cheyenne and work most effectively if care is taken to retain their original character. Starley Talbott and Michael Kassel know that is true. It shows in their book *A History Lover's Guide to Cheyenne*, which will lead you through the city while featuring its rich history.

The relative scale of all the distinctive buildings of the downtown and surrounding areas gives Cheyenne a unique personality. Familiar façades provide a sense of belonging. Built to last, older structures recall the pride of the owners and the community. This story about historic Cheyenne proves that the preservation and continued utilization of historic buildings and sites is necessary and desirable for sound community planning benefiting the welfare of its citizens. As monitored by the Cheyenne Historic Preservation Board, the careful encouragement of a program for restoration and reuse and an increased awareness that preserving historic structures makes economic as well as cultural sense are prevalent.

All have been touched with a degree of curiosity about historic buildings, the way in which they were built and how they have been used. This awareness continues to spread, and *A History Lover's Guide to Cheyenne* creates a momentum of support for our curiosity. Cheyenne's historic buildings are shells within which human interaction takes place and continues even when those who previously occupied these structures are long gone from this Earth. In my own experience as an architect for the Wyoming State Capitol Building restoration, a scribbled message on a plaster wall discovered during the process of investigation and examination, an old document found in a hidden corner where it was left unnoticed and the miscellaneous items discovered in forgotten roof and wall spaces all tell us something about those who have gone before and bring us closer to them.

When I arrived in Cheyenne in 2016 to become part of the team for the restoration of the Capitol Building, I was given a box of letters dating from 1887 written by John Feick, mostly to his wife, Lizzie. Feick was the on-site construction supervisor representing his firm Adam Feick & Bro. of Sandusky, Ohio, who had won the contract for constructing the Capitol. He describes his first day in Cheyenne as "snowing and blowing bad enough to scare a man to death." So, I wondered where I really was. I had just arrived after living in the beautiful mountain city of Prizren in the Republic of Kosovo, having spent the past five years in the United States Peace Corps, three of those years in Ukraine (2011–14), then on to Armenia and Kosovo (2015 and 2016). But as I got further into John Feick's letters, I could relate to his experiences when, eventually, his letters became incredibly positive about Cheyenne, its people and its culture. After over a year on the job, he wrote to Lizzie that "for some reason I hate to leave Cheyenne. I don't know why…but I hate to leave it." I agree with Feick's testament to Cheyenne's hospitality through its gracious people and important historic places.

We marvel at the craftsmanship of historic structures and sites built with ingenuity and inventiveness. *A History Lover's Guide to Cheyenne* is a perfect publication for visitors as well as residents to learn about the importance of Cheyenne's rich history. This narrative helps to ensure that the elements of our heritage are kept in the mainstream of contemporary life and are passed on to future generations to enjoy.

—Michael A. Dixon, FAIA/architect

Michael Dixon was the on-site architect and a historic preservation consultant for the Wyoming State Capitol Building during its restoration from 2016 until its grand reopening on July 10, 2019. During his time in Cheyenne, he was named an honorary member of the Cheyenne Historic Preservation Board, with which he worked to recognize and promote the city's unique heritage.

ACKNOWLEDGEMENTS

The authors are grateful for the many people who made the compilation of this book a reality. Without the writing, research and assistance of many historians, we could not have written this narrative.

Special thanks go to the staff and volunteers at the Wyoming State Archives, especially Suzi Taylor, Kathy Marquis and Jessica Cosgrove. Their ability to locate historical materials is remarkable.

We extend a hearty thank-you to Michael Dixon for his generosity in providing more than thirty of the magnificent color photos for our book. He took a genuine interest in Cheyenne's history and preservation while he served as the architect for the Wyoming State Capitol restoration.

The efforts of many people who provided information from personal collections are appreciated. We thank Sharon Field for her extensive research on Cheyenne history and a tour of the Cheyenne cemetery. We give special thanks to Steve Vandehei and Deidre Newman for information about the Humane Alliance Fountain. We appreciate local citizens who provided information about historic buildings and museums, with thanks to Bill Saunders, Bev Holmes, Jerry Bayne, Teresa Miller, Monica Asher Davis, Rick Ewig, Jim Ehernberger and others.

We are grateful for the staff at the Cheyenne Regional Airport, the staff at F.E. Warren Air Force Base and the staff at the Cheyenne Frontier Days™ Old West Museum for their assistance. We thank Roselyn Schliske for her dedicated service as a longtime instructor at Laramie County Community College and information about the college.

Special thanks to our acquisitions editor, Artie Crisp, and others at The History Press for their support and guidance.

Most importantly, we are grateful for our families and our spouses. Michael thanks his wife, Amy, who has been the wind beneath his wings blessing him with her encouragement and fortitude. Starley thanks her husband, Beauford Thompson, for his support in so many ways.

Starley thanks her co-author, Michael Kassel, for his important research and for his speaking ability, which first inspired her to delve further into the fascinating history of Cheyenne. Michael wishes to thank Starley Talbott, his co-author, for inspiring him to put into print that which inspired him about the people of Cheyenne and for opening doors he didn't think possible.

Lastly, we thank our readers and the many people who continue to inspire us with a love of history.

INTRODUCTION

Long before there was a state named Wyoming and a city named Cheyenne, Native Americans roamed the high plains east of the Rocky Mountains. The Plains tribes included Cheyenne, Arapahoe, Shoshone, Lakota and Crow.

Some of the earliest nonnative visitors to the area were fur traders and explorers in the 1830s. More travelers arrived during the 1840s, leading to increased contact with the Native Americans. Seeing a need for keeping peace in the region, the Plains tribes were invited to a treaty council in Fort Laramie in 1851, followed by additional councils. By the 1860s, people were traveling through what would become Wyoming headed for California and Oregon.

Though a few people settled along the migration trails, the largest population increase followed the establishment of the Union Pacific Railroad after the passage of Railroad Acts in 1862 and 1864. In the spring of 1867, two years before the territory of Wyoming was established, the laying of the tracks for the transcontinental railroad was approaching the high plains near what would become the city of Cheyenne.

Prior to 1867, the trip across the continent was arduous. In 1830, it took six months for covered wagons to travel from Missouri to the Pacific coast. By 1856, the route required twenty-one days by stagecoach. Trains were the next great venture in destroying space and time across the continent. The builders of the Union Pacific Railroad sought the easiest grade to pass through the Rocky Mountains and found that path through southern

Wyoming territory. This route was chosen because it formed a nearly straight line between Omaha and San Francisco. The city that would become Cheyenne was a major station on the railroad's route and was located at the foot of the lowest point across the Continental Divide at 8,200 feet.

On July 4, 1867, Grenville Dodge, chief engineer and head of the route survey for the Union Pacific Railroad, selected a site on Crow Creek as a division point for the railroad. At the same time, General C.C. Augur of the U.S. Army Department selected a site one mile west on Crow Creek as Fort D.A. Russell to protect the railroad workers. According to legend, the men in Dodge's survey group named the town Cheyenne, after the Native Americans who roamed the area. Following the construction of the railroad and the settling of the area, most of the Native Americans were pushed onto reservations.

By mid-July 1867, lots were being sold in the new town site. By the time the Union Pacific tracks arrived on September 10, 1867, Cheyenne was a tent town with a population estimated at four thousand. As winter approached, the tents were replaced by more permanent buildings and the population was estimated to be ten thousand. When spring arrived in 1868, the tracks moved on, and about half the population went with them. Due to the fluctuation of residents, the way buildings were constructed in a haphazard way and the rowdiness of the citizenry, Cheyenne was called a "Hell on Wheels" town. In its early years, the town had many bars and bawdyhouses contributing to its reputation. It was also dubbed with the title of "Magic City of the Plains" because it quickly became settled almost seemingly overnight.

The city's location on the first transcontinental railroad route was the major reason Cheyenne became an established town. The railroad remained an important economic center of the city and employed thousands of workers for many years. Cheyenne began to grow in other directions as well. In 1866, the first cattle were driven to Wyoming for grazing and shipping. Mercantile firms were established in the city, and soon many wealthy stock growers built homes in Cheyenne. Carey Avenue was lined with the mansions of merchants and cattlemen and became known as Millionaires Row.

In 1875, because of gold discoveries in Dakota Territory, the Wyoming territorial legislature approved a road from Cheyenne to Deadwood. Cheyenne was the closest city with a railroad link to the East, so it became the shipping point and banking center for the mines. The first Cheyenne to Deadwood stagecoach left Cheyenne in February 1876. The trip took three days with the coach traveling day and night, heavily guarded because of the gold cargo on board.

The harsh winter of 1886–87 brought a crash to the cattle business in southeastern Wyoming Territory. Cattle losses were estimated at 50 to 75 percent of the herds in the area. Some of the large cattle ranches went out of business and were replaced by smaller homesteaders. There was also a trend toward replacing cattle with sheep during the late 1800s.

Despite the economic setback, the city and the railroad continued to grow and thrive. The Union Pacific Railroad completed a handsome new depot in 1887 in order to promote the material interests of the city of Cheyenne. The Romanesque-style structure was built of red sandstone, and red oak lined the interior walls. A large portico was built under the 128-foot main tower, flanked by six large curved doorways.

As Wyoming added to the population and established other towns, the residents of Wyoming hoped to achieve statehood. Wyoming had quickly garnered national attention when the first territorial assembly met in Cheyenne in 1869 and granted all women above the age of twenty-one the right to vote. Wyoming Territory became the first place in the nation to grant women the voting franchise.

Francis E. Warren, territorial governor, advocated the need for public buildings. The territorial legislature passed a bill in March 1886 authorizing the construction of a capitol building. The company of Adam Feick & Bro. of Sandusky, Ohio, submitted the winning construction bid and broke ground on September 9, 1886. The exterior was of sandstone built in the French Renaissance architectural style and topped with a glittering dome that could be seen throughout the city. Wings were added in 1890 and 1917.

In 1889, the Wyoming Constitutional Convention met in the Territorial House Chamber of the new Capitol, where it reaffirmed the right of women to vote and included that right in the state constitution. On March 26, 1890, Wyoming's congressional delegate Joseph M. Carey introduced a bill calling for statehood. Despite some opposition, Wyoming became the forty-fourth state admitted to the Union on July 10, 1890.

A few short years later, the young city and state entered the twentieth century with confidence. For a time, Cheyenne was the center of many new developments. Cheyenne's role in aviation was significant. Beginning in 1920, Cheyenne's airport was one of the finest in the nation and served as a main stop on the first transcontinental airmail route. The airfield was the original home of Boeing Air Transport. It also served as an airplane modification center during World War II and the base for the United Air Lines Stewardess Training facility for several years.

Due to technology, Cheyenne eventually lost its aviation advantage to larger cities. The major tenant of the Cheyenne airfield today is the Wyoming Air National Guard. The city completed a brand-new airport terminal in 2018 and was recognized as the fastest-growing small airport in the nation in 2019.

From the earliest days of Cheyenne, the military base has played a significant role in the development of the city. Established as Fort D.A. Russell to defend the railroad in the 1800s, the fort continued to add to the fortunes of the city. The base has had three different names over the years: Fort D.A. Russell (1867–1929), Fort F.E. Warren (1930–49) and F.E. Warren Air Force Base (1949–present). Several historic structures built starting in 1885 are still in use at the base. The facility is designated a historic site with several historic districts and many structures listed in the National Register of Historic Places.

Cheyenne is blessed with many parks, monuments, recreational opportunities and a community college. It is home to the largest outdoor rodeo in the world and the celebration of its cowboy heritage each July with Cheyenne Frontier Days™.

The two most significant buildings in Cheyenne are the Union Pacific Railroad Depot and the Capitol, both designated as National Historic Landmarks. The city constructed many other important buildings as the town matured. Businesses, homes, schools, churches, museums and other enterprises contributed to the fascinating history of the high plains town named for the residents who first called the area home, the Cheyenne Native Americans.

Chapter 1

ROOTS AND WINGS

The high plains east of the Rocky Mountains, where the wind whistles through the prairie grass and the meadowlarks sing, was not yet a place where migrants planted roots a little more than a century ago. Native Americans, flora and fauna graced the countryside with their presence. A creek wound its way from the mountains slowly eastward into a gentle valley surrounded by ridges. This vast expanse of quiet prairie was about to burst into a frenzy of activity.

With a flurry of excitement, people began to flock to new towns all along the route being carved out for a new path headed west, a road of metal that would change the landscape forever. Thus begins the history of a city soon to be called Cheyenne.

THE RAILROAD

The United States Congress passed two Pacific Railroad acts in 1862 and 1864 leading to the construction of a transcontinental railroad. Two railroad companies were tasked with the opportunity to achieve such a grand achievement. The Union Pacific would lay track westward from Omaha, Nebraska, while the Central Pacific would establish the route eastward from Sacramento to Utah.

Surveyors were the first workers to arrive on the scene to calculate and mark the route covering two thousand miles of uncharted territory. As the railroad moved westward, Grenville Dodge, chief civil engineer of the Union Pacific Railroad, arrived at the site of the future city of Cheyenne on July 3, 1867. Dodge had earlier chosen the location, about five hundred miles west of Omaha, near a small stream named Crow Creek where the railroad would begin its ascent of the eastern slope of the Rocky Mountains. Dodge chose the site because it was the base of the lowest and easiest crossing of the Rocky Mountain Front Range. The crossing was later known as Sherman Pass, utilizing the extraordinary geographic feature known as the Gangplank. When Dodge arrived on July 3, the area was already teeming with activity from surveyors, military men and scouts. The following day, in celebration of July Fourth, the men made toasts and speeches to honor the plans for the city to be established at that location. Different versions of the celebration exist, but the conclusion was that the name of Cheyenne was chosen because of the local Native Americans in the area. However, the men were angry with the attacks the tribes had perpetrated on some of the workers.

At the same time, the site for an army post to be called Fort D.A. Russell was established. In addition, a quartermaster's depot named Camp Carlin was built as a supply point for all the forts in the region.

While Dodge supervised the survey of the townsite in early July, news spread of opportunities in the region, and thousands of people flocked to the area. The townsite was four miles square; streets and alleys were marked, and land was divided into city lots. The north–south streets were named for members of the survey party, including Dodge. By the time the tracks appeared on November 14, 1867, nearly ten thousand people had arrived. Soon, wooden buildings began to replace the tents that sheltered the first settlers. The city was described as "the magic city of the plains" due to the fact that it seemingly rose magically from the dusty expanse of the land.

Lots in the new town had sold quickly because Cheyenne had been selected as the winter terminus for the tracks. Cheyenne was to be a division point for the railroad where the Union Pacific would base all the operations of the Wyoming Division and be the junction of a major rail line to Denver and the ample precious minerals of the Rockies. However, the division point was still only a promise in late 1867. When spring arrived, the tracks moved on, and about half the population went with them. By the summer of 1868, Cheyenne was the point through which materials and supplies came for the six thousand men building tracks during the summer of 1868. Many of the town's most prosperous merchants got their start in these early years as wholesale grocers and general merchandise dealers.

Major repair facilities for the railroad were planned to be constructed in Cheyenne. However, several of those facilities were built in Laramie City instead of Cheyenne. For the next twenty years, locomotives were repaired in Laramie, often breaking down while climbing the slopes over the summit between Cheyenne and Laramie. Facilities were finally built in Cheyenne to accommodate more powerful locomotives.

The original stone roundhouse that was finally built in Cheyenne around 1890 was demolished and replaced in 1911. In 1931, the stalls were leveled and replaced with an updated twenty-stall roundhouse. Finally, in 1932, the Cheyenne roundhouse was completed with forty-eight stalls, forming a complete circle.

Beginning in 1889, the Union Pacific constructed shop buildings in Cheyenne including a machine shop, blacksmith shop, paint shop, tank and wheel shop and car shop. Cheyenne serviced the largest locomotives, including the Big Boys and the Challengers. Due to the steep grades at Sherman Hill, west of Cheyenne, and the rugged terrain of the Wyoming division, Cheyenne was home to the most powerful locomotives available. The Big Boy locomotive, the largest steam engine ever in operation, had to be maintained and repaired in Cheyenne.

The Union Pacific Railroad and shops. *J.E. Stimson Collection, Wyoming State Archives, Department of State Parks and Cultural Resources.*

Regular operation of steam power out of Cheyenne ended in July 1959. The roundhouse was not readily adaptable to the maintenance of diesel locomotives, so eventually most of the roundhouse was demolished. In addition, it was far easier for broken diesel locomotives to be shipped elsewhere for repair. A portion of the roundhouse with seven stalls was rehabilitated for Union Pacific's historic steam program in 1991. Over the ensuing years, several shops were no longer in use and were demolished. A shop used to serve the needs of the Union Pacific Heritage fleet is all that remains.

For many years during the decades of Union Pacific's operations in Cheyenne, a large group of skilled workers was employed at the Cheyenne shops to maintain the steam locomotives. The number of workers peaked just after World War II, when nine hundred folks worked in three shifts of three hundred for round-the-clock service. The large shop force, in addition to those working other Union Pacific jobs, made Union Pacific the largest employer in Cheyenne for many years.

The first Union Pacific passenger train from the east had arrived in Cheyenne on November 14, 1867. A wooden depot was built on the north side of the main line early in 1868. The building consisted of a waiting room, baggage room, mail room and express room. In October, a two-story hotel was erected east of the depot to accommodate overnight passengers. That structure burned down in 1872 and was replaced with a second hotel, which burned down in 1886 and was not replaced.

The cornerstone for an elegant new depot was laid on July 19, 1886, and the building was completed in November 1887. Designed by Henry Van Brunt in Romanesque style, and built of red and gray sandstone, the depot featured a main three-story section topped by a 128-foot clock tower. For political reasons, even though Cheyenne had a population of only around ten thousand, its vast wealth due to the cattle industry gave rise to the notion that the small town should have a depot commensurate with its phenomenal economic importance to the Union Pacific Railroad. In 1922, an addition was built on the east side of the depot. It housed a dining room operated by Union Pacific that operated until 1948, when it was closed and the space was converted to offices and a meeting hall.

The Union Pacific vacated the depot in 1990 and donated the structure to the Joint Powers Board. More than $4 million from various sources was used to stabilize and rehabilitate the building. The depot was transferred to the City of Cheyenne in 2001 and houses the chamber of commerce and depot board offices. The lobby is available for rent, and a depot museum and gift shop are located in the former baggage-express room. The depot was

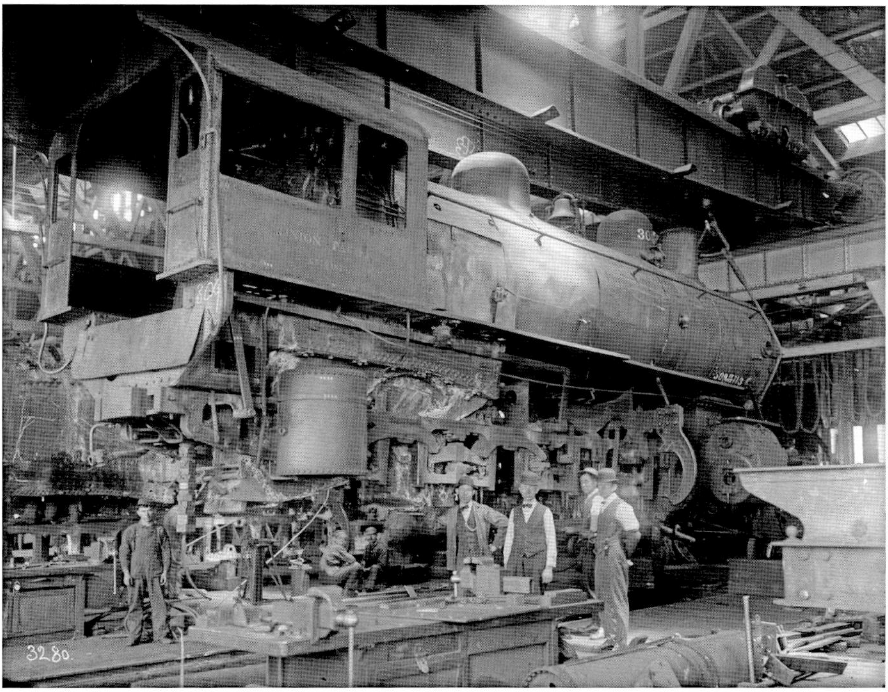

An interior view of the Union Pacific Railroad shops with workers in the boiler room. *J.E. Stimson Collection, Wyoming State Archives, Department of State Parks and Cultural Resources.*

designated a National Historic Landmark in 2006. The plaza in front of the depot hosts outdoor events and welcomes visitors to downtown Cheyenne.

The legacy of rail passenger service in Cheyenne had come to an end when Amtrak ended service to the city in the 1970s. There remains freight service, as trains rumble through the city. The small shops continue to provide maintenance. The steam shop has been busy restoring some of the famous steam engines known as the Big Boys. All of Union Pacific's Big Boys were retired by 1962. Engine Number 4002 was moved to Holliday Park, where it remains on display. Engine Number 4014 was restored and made a historical trip from Cheyenne to Ogden, Utah, in the spring of 2019. Folks lined the tracks for miles to see the wheels rotating and a fountain of steam billowing from the historic Big Boy.

The Union Pacific Railroad Depot in Cheyenne remains one of the city's most significant buildings, reminding the population that the railroad provided the roots for the city to grow.

The Union Pacific Railroad Depot showing a view of the track side of the depot. *J.E. Stimson Collection, Wyoming State Archives, Department of State Parks and Cultural Resources.*

THE STOCK GROWERS

The next important development for the economic future of Cheyenne was the birth of the cattle industry in the region. The first cattle were brought into Wyoming from Texas in 1866. During the summer and fall of 1867, cattle were driven into the Cheyenne area to provide meat for the railroad construction crews, the residents of the city and the troops at Fort Russell.

The high plains around Cheyenne provide arid grassland suitable for stock raising and some farming. The most successful of the early cattlemen was John Wesley Iliff, who established a cow camp on Crow Creek during the summer of 1867. The cattle industry boomed immediately, and Cheyenne became the cattlemen's headquarters. A group of pioneer cattlemen banded together in 1873 to form the Laramie County Stock Association. The group changed its name to the Wyoming Stock Growers Association in 1879.

As the cattle industry boomed, so did Cheyenne, becoming the wealthiest town per capita in the United States by 1884. Many of the stock growers built headquarters in Cheyenne, spending time at their ranches only during roundups. After cattle arrived in the area after being driven north from Texas, they were let loose to graze on federal and railroad lands. The big event of each year was the roundup, sponsored by the Wyoming Stock Growers Association. The newborn calves were rounded up and branded, and the herds were left to spend the summer feeding on grass. The cattle were left to fend for themselves in the winter. The year 1882 was the peak production year for cattle, bringing the ranchers a substantial profit.

Carey Avenue was lined with the mansions of merchants and cattlemen, and became known as Millionaires Row. Other livestock growers built homes throughout the city, and 17th Street was known as Cattlemen's Row.

The ranchers also established the Stock Growers National Bank in 1882 located in the Carey Block. The bank moved to its own building on Capitol Avenue and 17th Street in 1906.

Cheyenne's status as the cattlemen's headquarters was confirmed in 1880 with the establishment of the Cheyenne Club, initially and briefly called the Cactus Club. The club boasted a select membership representing

The Joseph Carey residence on Millionaires Row in Cheyenne no longer exists. *J.E. Stimson Collection, Wyoming State Archives, Department of State Parks and Cultural Resources.*

The Cheyenne Club was built in 1881 and no longer exists. The former Cheyenne Club, as shown in this photo, was the home of the chamber of commerce in the 1930s. *J.E. Stimson Collection, Wyoming State Archives, Department of State Parks and Cultural Resources.*

wealthy and elite stock growers from Wyoming, Montana and the Dakotas. It was soon the political and economic center of the cattle industry and Wyoming itself.

The Cheyenne Club building, designed by George Rainsford, was built on 17th Street and Warren Avenue in 1881. The building contained a full basement and a main floor with double parlors, a dining room, a library and a billiard room. Sleeping rooms were on the top floor with an observatory above. Two wine vaults and a kitchen were in the basement. An annual reception was staged each June. Nearly two hundred guests attended the 1887 reception, which was proclaimed the "Most Brilliant Social Event of the Season."

Soon after, in the winter of 1887, the stock growers suffered a major blow. The summer had been dry, leaving the already overstocked ranges with poor grass. This was followed by a cold, snowy and brutal winter. By spring, the losses were devastating, estimated to be 50 to 75 percent of a rancher's herd.

Most of the largest and best known of the stock growers quit the cattle business. Cattle prices continued to decline due to the poor condition of the remaining cattle and the low calf yield the following year. Many of the wealthy ranchers headquartered in Cheyenne sold their homes. The glorious years of the millionaire cattle barons and their Cheyenne Club came to an end near the close of the century.

In 1909, the former Cheyenne Club became headquarters for the Industrial Club of Cheyenne, which in 1927 became the chamber of commerce. The famous Cheyenne Club building was demolished in 1936.

THE CAPITOL

Established as a territory in 1868, Wyoming quickly garnered national attention when the first territorial assembly met in 1869 and granted all women above the age of twenty-one the right to vote. That move by the legislature made Wyoming the first territory in the United States where women were granted the voting franchise. The suffrage act was motivated by a number of factors, including enticing more women to the territory to increase the population, the desire to bring more voters into the population and genuine concerns that women should be allowed to vote.

Wyoming was still sparsely populated in 1886 when territorial governor Francis E. Warren spoke of a need for public buildings. The territorial legislature passed a bill authorizing the construction of a capitol at a cost not to exceed $150,000. Governor Warren signed the bill on March 4, 1886, and appointed the Capitol Building Commission.

The commission purchased a site on Hill Street, now Capitol Avenue, at a cost of $13,100. David W. Gibbs of Toledo, Ohio, was selected as the architect. The company of Adam Feick and Bro. of Sandusky, Ohio, submitted the winning construction bid of $131,275.13. The contractors broke ground on September 9, 1886.

Twenty-five-year-old John Feick, son of Adam Feick, was dispatched to Wyoming Territory to supervise the construction of the new capitol building. John wrote to his wife, Lizzie, after his arrival on February 2, 1887, telling her, "It is snowing and blowing bad enough to scare a man to death." In another letter, John told Lizzie, "There are very wealthy people living in this town, but they all look to me like Cow-boys." The young supervisor was quite lonely in his new outpost in Wyoming, though he eventually came to enjoy living in Cheyenne. As spring approached, John wrote to his wife about the excitement for the upcoming laying of the cornerstone.

John Feick's letter dated May 2, 1887, stated, "People are going crazy over the cornerstone....They are going to have a Barber Cue....The people of Cheyenne have appointed me on two committees." He wrote to Lizzie again on May 26 to describe the event, saying, "I suppose by this time you know what kind of a time we had at the laying of the Corner Stone, people expect to have a larger time on Decoration Day, I tell you this is a great country for excitement. People are more liberal & a nicer class of people than you find in the east."

There was a grand celebration for the laying of the cornerstone on May 18, 1887. Preparations for the celebration had taken weeks. A team of workers constructed a temporary cookhouse, tables were set up west of the Capitol and a fifty-foot-long barbecue pit was dug nearby. Following the dedication ceremony, the crowd thronged to the barbecue, where it dined on port, mutton, roast beef, bread, cornerstone pickles and lemonade.

After the copper box was placed under the cornerstone and the stone was in place, the crowd was addressed by several dignitaries, including Joseph M. Carey, Wyoming's delegate to the United States Congress, who gave a momentous speech on the early history of Wyoming. "The people should resolve that when the doors of the capitol shall swing open to receive the officers of the territory, that he who legislates for his private gain, that he who neglects to execute and fails to honestly administer the laws, shall be driven from its portals forever," declared Carey.

Shortly after the Capitol Building Commission submitted its final report on March 31, 1888, the territorial legislative assembly approved a bill for additional wings to be added to the Capitol. The second commission again selected David W. Gibbs as the architect but chose Moses P. Keefe for the construction, which was completed on April 4, 1890.

In 1889, the Wyoming Constitutional Convention met in the Territorial House Chamber of the new Capitol. The two-story room included a public balcony, a stained-glass lay light and a brilliant chandelier. The room is historical, for it was there that Wyoming reaffirmed the right of women to vote and included that right in the state constitution. The space also served as the chamber of the Wyoming Supreme Court and then housed the Legislative Service Office. Today, the historical Territorial House Chamber is once again restored as it was in 1889 and is a public meeting room. It is because of this room, and the inclusion of women's suffrage in Wyoming's constitution, that the Wyoming Capitol is designated a National Historic Landmark.

On March 26, 1890, Wyoming's congressional delegate Carey introduced a bill calling for statehood. Because of its low population (estimated at around

The Wyoming State Capitol around 1930. *J.E. Stimson Collection, Wyoming State Archives, Department of State Parks and Cultural Resources.*

sixty-two thousand in 1890), there was some opposition in the United States Congress to admittance. Despite those protests, including an objection to female suffrage, Wyoming became the forty-fourth state admitted to the Union on July 10, 1890.

The Capitol again needed additional space a few years later. The third Capitol Building Commission designated William Dubois of Cheyenne as the architect for the additions. Two new wings were constructed by the contractor John W. Howard and completed by March 15, 1917.

Changes occurred at the Capitol over the years to update and modernize the building. The most significant change began in 2016, when the Capitol was closed for three years for a complete renovation of it and adjacent office buildings that was completed in 2019. The Capitol Square Project comprised four interrelated components: rehabilitation and restoration of the Capitol; replacement, relocation and expansion of the central utility plant; remodeling and expansion of the underground passageway that connects the Capitol to the Herschler Building; and rehabilitation and expansion of the Herschler Building.

Some of the statues previously placed in the front of the Capitol were moved inside to keep them from deteriorating in the harsh Wyoming winter. Statues of Esther Hobart Morris and Chief Washakie were moved into the Capitol Extension near the future education center.

The exterior of the Capitol was updated, and some of the worn sandstone and masonry was replaced or repaired. The renovations upgraded the Capitol's Classical style and striking gold-leaf dome. The view from the Wyoming State Capitol south toward the Union Pacific Railroad Depot provides the link to Cheyenne's roots.

The city grew and changed. As the era of the late 1800s turned to the twentieth century, the city was ready to sprout its wings.

AIRMAIL

Because Cheyenne was established with the coming of the railroad, the city was a natural choice as a base for the development of moving the mail by a faster route. Trains were already part of the mail delivery system, but a new idea was to combine both rail and air service.

The builders of the Union Pacific Railroad had sought the easiest grade to pass through the Rocky Mountains and found that path through southern Wyoming. The route was also chosen because it formed a nearly straight line between Omaha and San Francisco and had the added benefit of being close to the mineral wealth of Colorado. Cheyenne, Wyoming, was a major station on the railroad's route and was located at the foot of the lowest point across the Continental Divide.

When the idea for a transcontinental airmail route was conceived, Cheyenne was considered as a natural division point for the airmail service. The city was chosen as a major station on the airmail route for many of the same reasons that it was deemed desirable by the builders of the railroad.

The plan for a transcontinental airmail service was considered difficult if not impossible by many. It had been proven that it was possible to fly airplanes across the continent when the U.S. Army Air Service conducted a Transcontinental Reliability and Endurance Test. One object of the air race was to demonstrate advances in aeronautical technology that could be used for peacetime purposes following World War I. However, Brigadier General William "Billy" Mitchell wanted to prove that an independent air force was necessary for the United States, and he wanted to garner support from the public to convince Congress to appropriate funds for such an endeavor.

United States airmail plane, model DH-4. *Wyoming State Archives, Department of State Parks and Cultural Resources.*

The Transcontinental Reliability Test was fraught with problems, delays and fatal crashes. However, the test did prove that airplanes could fly across the continent and provided a basis for the concept of a transcontinental airmail service. Otto Praeger, assistant postmaster, declared that the race had demonstrated the practicality of transcontinental airmail service, and he pressed for the adoption of such a route.

Airmail service nationwide was gradually adopted after early routes were established on the East Coast. The first itinerary between New York and Washington, D.C., of 218 miles provided one round trip daily beginning on May 15, 1918. Other routes were added, with three in operation during 1919 when daily mail service included eight planes flying around 1,900 miles each day. On May 15, 1920, the leg of the transcontinental route from Chicago to Omaha was established. The last leg of the transcontinental route from Omaha to San Francisco via North Platte, Cheyenne, Rawlins, Rock Springs, Salt Lake City, Elko and Reno was established on September 8, 1920.

The United States military provided airmail service in the beginning. The United States Post Office took over the operations in 1918 and continued to operate the airmail service until 1927, when they transferred airmail delivery to commercial airlines.

Chapter 2

BRANCHING OUT

The years 1867 to 1869 were formative for the city of Cheyenne. These years helped to form the perception that Cheyenne began as a "Hell on Wheels" town, including its share of rowdy citizens, houses of ill repute and some criminal activity.

The earliest structures were little more than tents or split-log shacks thrown together in a hurry to stake land claims and set up business. More substantial, though temporary, prefabricated buildings were brought by wagon from Julesburg, Colorado, in November 1867. This gave the town its "Hell on Wheels" moniker. Gradually, these buildings were disassembled and followed the progress of the railroad.

In subsequent decades, more prosperous and more diverse types of buildings were erected. In the city's second decade, 1877–87, larger houses spread north, toward the elaborate territorial Capitol building. Less substantial houses followed, extending to the north and east primarily. Workingman's cottages were built to the west and south of the core of the city.

The era of the cattlemen added to the romantic social scene of the city. Cheyenne also had a smaller, less splendid and more stable employer through the Union Pacific Railroad and the government.

Cheyenne's history includes an array of characters like ranchers, merchants, homesteaders, public officials, railroad workers and others. The architecture of the city reflects this history. Each building remaining adds a visual memory for Cheyenne, and each building lost takes part of Cheyenne with it.

HISTORIC HOMES

Carey Avenue

Carey Avenue, originally called Ferguson, was once called Millionaires Row because of the string of mansions that lined it. Other impressive homes lined the adjoining streets from 17th Street north to 25th Street. These mansions were built by Cheyenne pioneers who were early merchants and cattle ranchers, many of whom had come to Cheyenne to take positions in the territorial government.

The Joseph Carey Home

2119 Carey Avenue

Unfortunately, most of these grand mansions no longer exist. One of the most elaborate of these homes stood at 2119 Carey Avenue. This 1885 house in the Queen Anne style was the home of Joseph M. Carey.

Carey came to Cheyenne in 1869 to be the attorney general for the territory. He also ranched with his brother and was one of the founders of the Laramie County Stock Association. In 1871, he was appointed assistant justice of the territorial supreme court. He later served in Congress as territorial representative, as a United States senator in 1890 and Wyoming governor from 1911 to 1915.

The Idelman House

2323 Carey Avenue

One of the few mansions to survive on Carey Avenue is the Max Idelman House, across the street from the Wyoming Capitol. This brick and stone Queen Anne–style home was built in 1892 for Idelman, who was a wholesale liquor dealer along with his brother Abe.

The brothers operated the liquor business in the Idelman Building, constructed in 1884, at 16th Street and Carey Avenue (now the location of the Crown Bar). In the late 1800s, customers could walk among the barrels in front of the building and syphon off samples through a long tube and then purchase what they liked.

The Idelman house features towers and turrets, though a later addition obscures the first floor of the front façade. Years later, the home served as Schrader Funeral Home. It is now part of the Capitol Square complex.

Castle Dare

Another of the grand mansions on Carey Avenue that no longer remains is one known as the Castle Dare. The house was constructed around 1885 by Alexander Swan for his daughter Louise upon her marriage to Robert Van Tassell.

Often referred to as the Cattle King of the West, Swan came to the area in 1873 and established the vast Swan Land and Cattle Company. Van Tassell was also a substantial rancher when the couple married, and he continued to thrive and operate ranches in the area even after other ranches failed. The couple lived briefly in the Castle Dare mansion before they moved to another home.

Many of the large ranches, including the Swan Ranch, began to fail due to the disastrous winter of 1886–87. The Castle Dare house was sold for back taxes to banker David Dare. Eventually, Dare also failed in his financial affairs, and the house reverted to a man named Bradley, who had never been paid for his work when the castle was first constructed. The house had

This grand mansion, sometimes called Castle Dare or Bradley's Castle, was constructed in 1885 and no longer exists. *J.E. Stimson Collection, Wyoming State Archives, Department of State Parks and Cultural Resources.*

a number of residents and a variety of uses as a rooming house, mortuary and the IOOF Lodge. The house was demolished in 1962 to make way for expansion of county buildings.

The Van Tassell Home and Carriage Barn

921 East 17th Street

Robert Van Tassell and Louisa Swan were married in 1886. They may or may not have lived in the Castle home that Alexander Swan gave his daughter for a wedding gift. Alexander Swan could not afford to pay for the house, and it reverted back to the builder.

Robert and Louisa moved to a home at 921 East 17th Street owned by J.B. Thomas, and eventually they purchased the home in 1892. The property included a home and a carriage barn, designed by architect George Rainsford.

The Van Tassell home and carriage barn. The carriage barn was moved to Holliday Park and is the home of the Cheyenne Art Guild. *Wyoming State Archives, Department of State Parks and Cultural Resources.*

Van Tassell continued to ranch and was involved in various other commercial concerns. The couple enjoyed prominence among Cheyenne society. They attended the inauguration of Francis E. Warren as territorial governor in April 1889, among other important events for the next several years.

However, Robert and Louisa divorced in 1912. In 1913, Van Tassell married Maude Bradley, the daughter of Robert Bradley, who had built the castle that was to have been for Van Tassell and Louisa Swan.

Robert Van Tassell died in 1931, and four of his ranch properties and the mansion at East 17th Street were willed to his widow, Maude. She donated the properties to the Children's Hospital of Denver, Colorado. The Van Tassell Carriage Barn, however, was moved to Holliday Park, where it is the home of the Cheyenne Artists Guild and is in the National Register of Historic Places.

Willis Van Devanter House

802 East 18th Street

Willis Van Devanter, a twenty-five-year-old attorney, moved to Cheyenne from Indiana in 1884. He opened a law practice in the city after learning that his brother-in law, John W. Lacy, had been appointed as chief justice of Wyoming Territory.

Van Devanter and his wife, Dollie, settled in Cheyenne in a home on East 18th Street in the Rainsford Historic District of the city.

As his law practice developed, Van Devanter often traveled by horseback or stagecoach to appear in court in remote locations throughout Wyoming. He was interested in representing people involved in the livestock and railroad occupations. One of his clients was the Swan Land and Cattle Company, which held large sections of land and grazed cattle in southeastern Wyoming.

The young attorney also offered his assistance to Territorial Governor Francis E. Warren. The two men became lasting friends.

One of Van Devanter's early achievements for the State of Wyoming was assisting in the bill authorizing funds for the construction of the Capitol Building and funds to establish the University of Wyoming. It is said that he was proud of the role he played in the creation of the Capitol Building and the university. He also assisted in revising statutes creating Wyoming's new state constitution and laws.

The Willis Van Devanter home. *Wyoming State Archives, Department of State Parks and Cultural Resources.*

Other achievements in Van Devanter's law career were serving as city attorney for Cheyenne in 1887 and being elected to serve in the territorial legislature in 1888. He was a staunch Republican and served on Francis E. Warren's inaugural committee for his reappointment as territorial governor in 1889.

In the same year of 1889, Van Devanter became chief justice of the Wyoming Supreme Court. He presided in the First District overseeing cases in Laramie, Converse, Crook and later Weston Counties.

After his service in Wyoming, Van Devanter became the assistant attorney general for the United States in 1897, a position he held until 1903. He then became the United States Circuit Court judge for the Eighth Judicial District, consisting of Minnesota, Iowa, Missouri, Arkansas, Kansas, Nebraska, South Dakota, North Dakota, Wyoming, Colorado, Utah, Oklahoma and New Mexico.

On December 15, 1910, Van Devanter was appointed to a position on the Supreme Court of the United States. He was the only attorney from

Wyoming to serve on the Supreme Court, from which he resigned in 1937. He died at the age of eighty-one on February 8, 1941, and was buried in Washington, D.C.

Keefe Buildings

The area just to the north of the Capitol was home to many state officials. Moses P. Keefe lived at 210 West 27th Street. Keefe was one of Cheyenne's most active contractors and builders. He is best known for his construction of the first two wings added to the Capitol.

Keefe was involved in the building of the Idelman Mansion, the West Side School, the Majestic Building, First Methodist Church, St. Mark's Episcopal Church, St. Mary's Cathedral and the Wyoming Trust and Savings Building. He also constructed many buildings at Fort D.A. Russell.

One of Keefe's most impressive projects is Keefe Row, a National Register Historic District, located along 22nd Street and Evans Avenue. This group of nine houses was designed by architect J.P. Julien and constructed by Keefe between 1892 and 1900. The houses are all of red brick, one and one-half stories tall and topped by gable roofs. Each of these Queen Anne–style houses features a spindle post porch and gable detailing.

The Keefe Cottages on Evans Avenue. *Wyoming State Archives, Department of State Parks and Cultural Resources.*

Nettford Apartments

Arthur C. Kingsford and his wife, Nettie, owned the Nettford Apartments at 215 East 18th Street. The Georgian red brick structure with white columns on the front was built in 1911 and contains twelve apartments.

Kingsford was a foreman on the Union Pacific Railroad and secretary of the Railway Employees Building and Loan Association.

The apartment building still stands today and can be viewed from the outside when taking a walking tour of historic downtown Cheyenne.

Whipple-Lacey Home

302 East 17th Street

The Whipple-Lacey House, at 302 East 17th Street, is one of the historic mansions remaining in Cheyenne. The house was built by Ithamar C. Whipple, one of Cheyenne's pioneer merchants, in the early 1880s.

Whipple owned a wholesale grocery business in historic downtown Cheyenne. In 1884, he joined with other pioneer businessmen to form the Union Mercantile Company. He was also involved in banking and ranching and became a member of the Wyoming Stock Growers Association in 1879. The house was sold to John W. Lacey, a Cheyenne lawyer, around 1893.

John Lacey was appointed chief justice of the Wyoming Territory Supreme Court in 1884, where he served for two years before returning to private practice. He served as chief counsel for the Wyoming Stock Growers Association and the Union Pacific Railroad. Lacey lived in the two-story brick house until his death in 1936. The house is listed in the National Register of Historic Places.

Nagle and Warren Mansion

222 East 17th Street

Erasmus Nagle was the chairman of the Capitol Building Commission in 1886. He was also a rancher, an officer of the Wyoming Stock Growers Association and a well-known Cheyenne merchant.

Nagle's first house at 216 East 17th Street is one of the earliest brick houses in the city. Nagle decided he needed a larger home, so right next door he built a grander home out of stone rejected for use in the State Capitol because the stone was considered "too soft." The exterior of the Queen Anne–style home eventually had to be covered with stucco when

The Nettford Apartments on East 18th Street. *Wyoming State Archives, Department of State Parks and Cultural Resources.*

The Whipple-Lacey residence on East 17th Street. *Wyoming State Archives, Department of State Parks and Cultural Resources.*

the stone began to deteriorate. Nagle died in 1890, and his widow remained in the house until 1910.

The Nagle House was purchased by Frances E. Warren, one of Cheyenne's most distinguished citizens, in 1915. Like Nagle, Warren came to Cheyenne in 1868 as a merchant, but he soon became involved in a variety of interests, including government.

Warren established the Warren Mercantile Company and replaced it with the Warren Emporium at the location currently known as the Cheyenne Depot Plaza. The Emporium was demolished in the 1920s. He also operated the Warren Livestock Company with holdings of goats, cattle, sheep and horses. The Warren Livestock Company is one of the early ranches that has survived to the present day.

Warren is best known for his role as a public servant. He was appointed territorial governor in 1885 and was the first elected state governor of Wyoming in 1890. He resigned shortly thereafter to become one of Wyoming's first senators, a position he would keep for nearly thirty years. Fort D.A. Russell was renamed Fort F.E. Warren upon the senator's death in 1930.

The home is now called the Nagle-Warren Mansion and is a bed-and-breakfast establishment. Most of the original interior has been preserved. The building is listed in the National Register of Historic Places.

The original Erasmus Nagel residence on East 17th Street. *Wyoming State Archives, Department of State Parks and Cultural Resources.*

The second Nagel residence was constructed of stone that had been rejected for use in the building of the state Capitol. It later became known as the Nagel-Warren Mansion after Francis E. Warren purchased the home. *J.E. Stimson Collection, Wyoming State Archives, Department of State Parks and Cultural Resources.*

Rainsford Historic District

The Rainsford Historic District is named after architect George D. Rainsford. He came to Wyoming in the 1870s to raise horses at his Diamond Ranch, located northwest of Cheyenne.

Rainsford had been trained in architecture in Europe and New York City. He designed his ranch buildings and his home at 702 East 18th Street in Cheyenne. He also designed many other buildings in the Rainsford Historic District. All of his designs are variations on the Shingle style.

One of the homes in the district is the Corson Queen Anne Cottage. Samuel Corson arrived from Scotland in 1883 to build this home from plans by architect George Rainsford, using Rainsford's signature fish scale shingles on the exterior.

The Corson Queen Anne Cottage on East 18th Street, featuring the Rainsford-style fish scale shingles, is now the home of Danielmark's Brewery. *Wyoming State Archives, Department of State Parks and Cultural Resources.*

Many of the homes in the Rainsford District, located between historic downtown and Holliday Park, had been designed for area ranchers. Many of the ranchers' homes were not mansions but were smaller because they were often used for only part of the year. After the early cattle industry faded, these small houses were affordable for government employees and officials, merchants and others.

Lakeview Historic District

The Lakeview District is located north of the Rainsford District and east of the Capitol. It is named for the cemetery to the east of the district. The Lakeview- and Rainsford-area homes have similar characteristics and development patterns.

One of the Lakeview District's most important homes is the Sir Morton Frewen House at 506 East 23rd Street. The Gothic Revival–style house dates to 1880. Morton Frewen was a prominent area rancher, and he kept a relay of wagons he used to transport guests to his 76 Ranch headquarters near Buffalo, Wyoming.

Other homes in the district included homes primarily occupied by government and railroad employees.

Esther Hobart Morris House

2114 Warren Avenue

Esther Hobart Morris lived in the small hipped-roof cottage at 2114 Warren Avenue from 1890 to 1902. The house was later occupied by architect William Dubois, who designed many of Cheyenne's houses and buildings.

Esther Morris previously lived in South Pass City, Wyoming. She was the first woman in the nation to hold the office of justice of the peace when she was appointed for the position in South Pass City in 1870.

Morris played a minor role in the fight for women's suffrage when Wyoming's territorial legislature approved a bill allowing women the right to vote in 1869, making Wyoming the first territory to do so. When Wyoming became a state in 1890, the right for women to vote was included in the state's constitution. Esther Morris participated in the festivities celebrating statehood. Morris spent her later years residing in her home on Warren Avenue, only a few blocks from the State Capitol. A historic marker denoting the "National Votes for Women Trail" was placed on the grounds of the former Morris home in August 2021. The marker honors Morris as an advocate of votes for women in Wyoming.

A statue of Esther Hobart Morris graced the Wyoming Capitol grounds and represents Wyoming in the United States Capitol Statuary Hall. Her statue at the Wyoming Capitol was moved inside the building following the renovation of the Capitol that was completed in 2019.

Nellie Tayloe Ross and William Ross House

Nellie Tayloe Ross and William B. Ross occupied a two-story wood frame house on East 17th Street from 1908 until 1922.

William Ross, a Cheyenne attorney, was elected governor in 1922, and the family moved into the Governor's Mansion at 300 East 21st Street in 1923. Governor Ross died from a ruptured appendix on October 2, 1924.

Nellie Tayloe Ross was elected on November 9, 1924, to fill her husband's unexpired term. She was the first woman to serve as governor of any state in the United States, and she served for two years.

After Ross lost her bid for reelection, she became a speaker on the Chautauqua Lecture Circuit. Franklin Roosevelt appointed her director of the U.S. Mint in 1933, a position she held for twenty years. As such, she was the first woman to direct a major federal institution.

Nellie Tayloe Ross died in 1978 at the age of 101 and is buried next to her husband in Lakeview Cemetery in Cheyenne.

Historic Governor's Mansion

300 East 21st Street

The Wyoming state legislature authorized the construction of the Wyoming Governor's Manson and appropriated $3,000 for the purchase of land and $37,000 for construction. The red brick Georgian Colonial–style building at 300 East 21st Street was dedicated in January 1905.

The first floor of the mansion consists of an entrance foyer, large reception hall, library, drawing room, study, formal dining room, breakfast room, kitchen, pantry, service porch and sitting room. Bedrooms compose the second and third floors. The mansion's basic design and structure have remained the same throughout the years with a few modifications.

After this structure housed the governor and first families for more than seventy years, a new Governor's Mansion was constructed in north Cheyenne in the 1970s at the location that had been the American Legion Park near Interstate 25. The historic mansion needed updated security and additional amenities for modern living. The public spaces were too small for events and receptions, and the private spaces were not adequately separated from the public space.

The original mansion underwent several restorative events to return it to its former glory. The Historic Governor's Mansion, in the National Register of Historic Places, is now a museum that is open for tours and other special events.

THE HISTORIC DOWNTOWN AND BUSINESS DISTRICT

The historic district of early downtown Cheyenne was located near the Union Pacific Depot and the railroad tracks. This was the area where the shipping, supply and entertainment of the town was located during the period from 1867 to 1876.

The city continued to grow and develop throughout the years. The main portion of the central business district is listed in the National Register of Historic Places and is called the Downtown Historic District. Areas designated as the North Central Business District and the West District are also included as part of Cheyenne's historic area.

First National Bank Building

210 West 16th Street

The First National Bank Building, erected in 1882, was one of the first substantial structures in the historic district. The three-story edifice was constructed of brick, stone and iron at a cost of $17,000.

The bank occupied the first floor. The second floor was divided into six offices. The third floor was occupied by the F.E. Warren Company.

The Phoenix Block

16th Street and Capitol Avenue

Erected in 1882 at a cost of $35,000, the Phoenix Block remains one of the substantial early buildings occupying the downtown historic district. The three-story building boasted a complete system of plumbing, water and gas available in all rooms.

The Phoenix Block, 1882, when the building served as the Baker and Johnson Grocers business. *Wyoming State Archives, Department of State Parks and Cultural Resources.*

On the ground floor were three stores facing Capitol Avenue and two stores facing 16th Street. On the second floor were seventeen offices. The third floor held twenty-seven family rooms. The front of the building was made of cut stone, pressed brick and iron. Today, the building is the home of a western clothing store.

The Commercial Building

North Side of 16th Street between Capitol and Carey Avenues

The Commercial Building was constructed in 1883. It originally housed a wholesale liquor store and a harness and saddlery shop on the main floor. The upstairs portion of the building contained office and room rentals.

The J.S. Collins Harness and Saddlery Company gained appreciation in an 1887 edition of the *Cheyenne Daily Sun* as a place that "offers to horsemen a very fine and varied line of turf goods. They have made especial preparation for supplying this trade and can afford the owners of running and trotting flyers better opportunities to get what they want than ever before presented to them. In English saddlery goods, they have a particularly fine line."

The Commercial Building gained notoriety when U.S. marshal Joe LeFors met with Tom Horn in an office on the second floor behind a bay window on January 11, 1902. Horn had been employed by a number of ranchers to work as a stock detective in finding cattle rustlers. He was known to have killed a few suspected cattle thieves in the late 1890s. Horn was suspected in the murder of fourteen-year-old Willie Nickell at Iron Mountain, northwest of Cheyenne, on July 18, 1901, allegedly to keep the boy from reporting Horn's presence in the area. Marshal LeFors secured a confession to the murder from Horn at his office in the Commercial Building, though it was said that Horn was in a drunken stupor at the time. Horn was hanged for the murder of the young boy in Cheyenne on November 20, 1903, though there remains lingering doubt as to who actually murdered Willie Nickell.

In later years, the ground floor was occupied by the Trail Café and the Western Ranchmen Outfitters store. It is now the location of the Wyoming Home gift shop.

The Atlas Theater

213 West 16th Street

The original Atlas Building was constructed in 1887 and is listed in the National Register of Historic Places. Several business enterprises occupied the building over the years, and extensive remodeling occurred over time.

The top floors of the structure were used for office space from 1887 to 1908, and the bottom floor was a tea shop. In 1908, the building was remodeled to include a theater at the rear of the building. The front area included a soda fountain and candy shop.

The Atlas Theater remained in operation until the end of 1929. In 1930, the theater reopened as the Strand, and the upper floors were used as the Strand Hotel.

In the early 1960s, the Atlas Building held the Pink Pony Night Club. Following the closing of the club, the building lay vacant for several years. The Cheyenne Little Theatre Players reopened the building in 1966. Today, events are held at the historic Atlas Theater throughout the year.

The Tivoli Building

301 West 16th Street

The Tivoli Building was constructed in the 1880s on the prominent southwest corner of 16th Street and Carey Avenue. The building was owned by Warren Richardson, who maintained an office on the second floor of the building.

The Tivoli Building housed a restaurant and beer parlor that opened in 1892. The building was filled with massive oak furnishings and was said

The Tivoli Building all decked out for a Cheyenne celebration. *Wyoming State Archives, Department of State Parks and Cultural Resources.*

to be the latest and most modern to be found in the United States. It has been the home to various enterprises throughout the years, including the Cheyenne Chamber of Commerce.

The Telephone Building

1623 Capitol Avenue

The Rocky Mountain Bell Telephone Company opened its offices in this building in 1906. Rocky Mountain Bell and the Mountain States Telephone Company occupied the building until the late 1920s.

Various other owners have occupied this building over the years, including its use as a hotel, shops and the Royal Optical Company.

The Majestic Building

16th Street at Capitol Avenue

William R. Dubois was the architect for the Majestic Building that opened in 1907 as the First National Bank. The bank closed in 1924, and the building was redesigned as an office and store complex.

The ground floor has included a barbershop, souvenir and gift shops, a museum and the Capitol Avenue entrance to the famed Peacock Alley of the Plains Hotel.

The Capitol Avenue and Paramount Theatre

1607 Capitol Avenue

The building that is called the Paramount Theatre was built in 1905 and was originally called the Capitol Avenue Theatre. The Capitol Avenue Theatre was damaged by fire in 1915. The building was remodeled in the 1930s as a movie theater and renamed the Paramount. A fire destroyed most of the Paramount Theatre building in 1981, leaving only the west-facing front of the building containing offices and retail space.

Jon and Renee Jelinek purchased the coffee shop in the Paramount building in 2013. They also purchased the entire Paramount building and the connecting Majestic Building. Both buildings had been designed by architect William Dubois.

The Jelineks opened the Paramount Ballroom and café in 2017. They also acquired the Lincoln Theatre on Central Avenue in 2018.

The Lincoln Theatre, around 1930, on Central Avenue. *Wyoming State Archives, Department of State Parks and Cultural Resources.*

The Lincoln Theatre

1615 Central Avenue

William Dubois was the architect for the Lincoln Theatre. Opened in March 1927, the Art Deco–style building featured a main level and a balcony in the interior. The building was touted as being equal in size and quality to any theater in the Rocky Mountain region.

The Lincoln has been remodeled several times throughout the years and hosted a variety of venues, including a movie theater.

The present owners, John and Renee Jelinek, have honored the historic structure of the Lincoln while updating such features as lighting and sound equipment. The venue has a capacity of 1,200 people, and future plans include live concerts and other entertainment.

The Plains Hotel

1600 Central Avenue

One of the grandest historic buildings in Cheyenne is the Plains Hotel, where the grand opening featured a formal dinner party and dance on March 10, 1911. The hotel was one of the first major accommodations created to cater to the growing auto tourism trade. Every room had a telephone, and almost all of the rooms had private bathrooms.

The five-story hotel boasted one hundred original rooms, each furnished with sumptuous carpets and draperies. The lobby received daylight through a skylight, modeled after the planets that were then known, highlighting the tile and mahogany floor. Leather furniture graced the lobby.

Throughout the years, the Plains Hotel was a favorite gathering place for locals and visitors. The Wigwam Lounge was a favorite meeting place for stewardesses who attended the United Air Lines stewardess training school in Cheyenne from 1947 to 1961. The stewardesses would be brought to downtown Cheyenne on weekend evenings, sometimes by an elderly bowlegged cowboy driving a station wagon. The ladies would be dropped

The Plains Hotel, around 1911. *Wyoming State Archives, Department of State Parks and Cultural Resources.*

off on Capitol Avenue, where they entered the Plains through an alley called Peacock Alley. The alley gained its name from both the glamorous stewardesses and the glamorous women who used to perform at the nearby Paramount Theatre, who used the corridor as a discreet entrance.

The Plains was bursting with excitement each year when thousands of visitors descended on Cheyenne during Cheyenne Frontier Days™. Cowboys and Native Americans were often honored guests at the Plains Hotel.

A fifty-room addition was added to the Plains Hotel in 1928. The hotel still remains in business in historic downtown Cheyenne. There are ongoing efforts to preserve and renovate the venerable structure.

The Gleason and Grier Building

1601 Central Avenue

Francis E. Warren was the owner of the Gleason Building, erected in 1911 and designed by architect William R. Dubois. The building was occupied by the Gleason Mercantile Company, supplying household furnishings. Herbert Gleason, president of the company, also offered funeral and embalming services.

In 1948, the business was purchased by R.S. Grier and became the Grier Furniture Company, operating for many years. Numerous enterprises have occupied the building during the past five decades.

Union Pacific Hospital

303 East 17th Street

The Union Pacific Hospital was built in 1903 for the company doctor as a residence and small hospital. It was necessary to have a hospital close to the Union Pacific tracks to attend to employees of the railroad.

The historic building is now occupied by Deselms Fine and Custom Framing Business.

Cheyenne Opera House

Capitol Avenue and 17th Street

The Cheyenne Opera House opened in May 1882 at the corner of 17th and Hill Streets (now Capitol Avenue). The opera house was dedicated to the promotion of literature, art, science, music and other interests.

The structure included a theater, territorial library, banquet hall, ballroom and dressing rooms. Many well-known people performed at the opera house during its twenty years of operation.

The building was sold in 1906 to Joseph and Robert Carey, who remodeled the structure to include space for offices and stores. A fire had destroyed the theater section of the building in 1902. The opera house was demolished in the 1960s, leaving another historic building in Cheyenne lost to history.

The Warren Emporium

Capitol Avenue and 16th Street

Francis E. Warren built the Warren Emporium in 1884. At that time, it was the largest retail structure in Cheyenne. The Emporium featured furniture, carpets, glassware and many other items. The company shipped its products to towns throughout Wyoming.

The Chicago, Burlington and Quincy (CB&Q) Railroad used the facility as its depot for many years into the twentieth century. The Burlington Bus Depot occupied the space after the original Emporium was demolished in the 1920s.

The area is now the location of the Depot Plaza. The plaza is used for events throughout the year. The eight-foot-tall boots that decorate the plaza were painted by local artists and reflect various themes related to Cheyenne. Other boots are located in several locations of the city.

Hynds Building

16th Street and Capitol Avenue

The Hynds Building was completed in 1922 for Harry P. Hynds, a prominent Cheyenne businessman and philanthropist. The architect for the building was William R. Dubois.

The structure is on the site of the famed Inter-Ocean Hotel, which burned down in 1916. As a result of the fire, the Hynds Building was constructed completely out of nonflammable materials, making it the first fireproof structure of its type in Wyoming. Businesses that have occupied the building include the American National Bank, Cheyenne National Bank and office space.

Hynds came to Cheyenne in 1882 and worked in his trade as a blacksmith for several years. He owned saloons in Cheyenne and leased the Plains Hotel

The Cheyenne Opera House, opened in 1882 on Capitol Avenue, was demolished in the 1960s. *Wyoming State Archives, Department of State Parks and Cultural Resources.*

The Warren Emporium, shown in the lower right corner of this photo, no longer exists. It was located at the corner of Capitol Avenue and 16th Street, where the Cheyenne Depot Plaza is now located. *Wyoming State Archives, Department of State Parks and Cultural Resources.*

The Hynds Building, built of steel and concrete in 1922 to be completely fireproof, replaced the Inter-Ocean Hotel that burned down. *J.E. Stimson Collection, Wyoming State Archives, Department of State Parks and Cultural Resources.*

when it opened in 1911. He is remembered for his generosity to groups and citizens of Cheyenne.

The first floor of the historic Hynds Building is currently occupied by several art galleries and other small business enterprises.

Boyd Building

1720 Carey Avenue

Built in 1912 by the Citizens National Bank, the Boyd Building has held many different business enterprises. The bank closed in 1925, and H.N. Boyd purchased the building.

Businesses that have occupied this building include office space, the headquarters of the Internal Revenue Service agents responsible for overseeing Prohibition enforcement, a drugstore, a women's clothing store, a gift shop, a coffee shop and a bookstore.

The original Dinneen Garage and Filling Station. *Wyoming State Archives, Department of State Parks and Cultural Resources.*

Dinneen's Garage

400 West 16th Street

The red brick edifice with its two familiar towers is a prominent Cheyenne landmark built in 1927 to serve the many travelers on the Lincoln Highway. It was designed for William E. Dinneen, who began an automobile business in Cheyenne in 1906.

During Dinneen's lifetime, the business was open twenty-four hours a day. He was very proud of Cheyenne and felt that travelers on the Lincoln Highway, as well as his regular customers, should receive first-class treatment.

The Dinneen family operated the garage for many years, selling several makes of automobiles. Today, the building has been remodeled and contains a restaurant and other businesses.

The Asher Wyoming Company

15th Street and Thomes Avenue

The Asher Wyoming Company served Cheyenne and southeastern Wyoming businesses for forty years. The warehouse building was constructed in 1932 in the historic railroad district of the city.

A spur from the Union Pacific Railroad tracks used to come right up to a dock on the side of the building. Boxes of groceries were unloaded at the dock and moved into the warehouse. Trucks were then loaded and dispatched to mom-and-pop grocery stores, restaurants and institutions throughout the city and other small towns in southeastern Wyoming, western Nebraska and northern Colorado.

The officers of the company were Samuel Asher, president; Herbert Kingham, vice president; and Lester Asher, secretary-treasurer. Lester was the son of Samuel and was also in charge of keeping the trucks in running order.

Monica Asher Davis, daughter of Lester, recalls visiting the warehouse with her father and siblings occasionally. She described the building as a large, rough building located in a rough neighborhood. She fondly

The Asher Wyoming Warehouse in the 1930s. *Wyoming State Archives, Department of State Parks and Cultural Resources.*

remembers riding in a cardboard box down a wooden slide from the second floor to the first floor. The slide was used to send boxes of merchandise within the building. The children also were allowed to ride with their father in the open cage elevator, which Monica says was "scary."

The business was liquidated in 1972. Gordon Campbell purchased the building and remodeled and repurposed the space for other uses. There are currently several shops and artist spaces being used within the former warehouse.

GOVERNMENT BUILDINGS AND INSTITUTIONS

Veterans Administration Center

2360 East Pershing Boulevard

The Veterans Hospital was constructed in 1934. Since opening day, the facility has undergone many changes. In 1946, the hospital was redesignated as the Cheyenne Veterans Administration Center. The grounds around the fifty-acre facility are maintained with lawns and trees. The trees serve as a windbreak, making the grounds tranquil even in the depths of winter.

Supreme Court Building

2301 Capitol Avenue

William R. Dubois was the architect of the Supreme Court Building, constructed in 1936. Leslie Miller was the Wyoming governor during the construction period. The building is one of the finest examples of government structures built by the Public Works Administration.

Dubois is considered Wyoming's premier architect. He came to Cheyenne when he was twenty-two years old. His first assignment in the city was to supervise construction of the Carnegie Library. He became a prominent citizen of Cheyenne and served as a member of the Wyoming State House and Senate for ten years. He married the daughter of newspaper editor E.A. Slack. Dubois designed many of Cheyenne's buildings, including the Plains Hotel, the Elks Club, the Stock Growers National Bank and numerous schools and residences. His grandson William R. Dubois is a Cheyenne historian and author.

McCormick Junior High School/Emerson State Office Building

2001 Capitol Avenue

This building originally was the McCormick Junior High School, containing thirty-eight classrooms, a gymnasium and a library. The building also contained an auditorium with a seating capacity of 1,222, used for many years as Cheyenne's civic auditorium.

William R. Dubois was the architect for the building that was completed in 1929. The facility was purchased by the State of Wyoming upon the completion of a new junior high school in 1975. The office building was then named in honor of former governor Frank C. Emerson.

City and County Building

19th Street and Central Avenue

William R. Dubois was the architect for the City and County Building that was completed in 1919 on the site of the first Laramie County Courthouse that had been built in 1874.

A monument in the form of a cowboy boot stands outside this building explaining the "Saga of Tom Horn." Horn was hanged at this location on November 20, 1903, for the alleged murder of a young man. Several plaques also tell about prominent citizens of Cheyenne.

Today, the area includes several government buildings for the city and county.

The City and County Building. *J.E. Stimson Collection, Wyoming State Archives, Department of State Parks and Cultural Resources.*

Cheyenne Civic Center

510 West 20th Street

Built in 1981, the Cheyenne Civic Center offers various entertainment activities, lectures, celebrations and other events. The west side of the structure holds municipal offices for the City of Cheyenne.

The goal of the Civic Center is to provide a community performing arts center dedicated to providing Cheyenne with a top-quality venue in which to present the arts. The building is well designed for its supreme sound quality.

SCHOOLS

Cheyenne Public High Schools

Cheyenne Public Schools Administration Building

The first Cheyenne High School was constructed in 1890 at Central Avenue and 22nd Avenue. The building served as a high school until 1922.

The new Cheyenne Public High School opened in 1922 on House Avenue and served as a high school until 1976. As the city grew, the Cheyenne School Board determined that it was necessary to have two public high schools.

The Cheyenne Public High School was renamed Central High School, and a second high school named East High School was built in 1961. A new Central High School was opened in north Cheyenne in 1976. Additional high schools are Triumph High School and South High School. Several additions have been made to the building at 2810 House Avenue that became the Administration Building for the Cheyenne Public School System.

Churchill School

510 West 29th Street

Churchill School, constructed in 1911, was named for James Churchill, superintendent of Cheyenne schools for many years. The architect was William R. Dubois.

Students from Fort D.A. Russell (F.E. Warren Air Force Base) attended Churchill School for many years.

Gibson Clark School

28th Street and House Avenue

The Gibson Clark School, built in 1920, served as an elementary school for many years and later became part of the Central High School complex.

The school was named for an early-day Cheyenne attorney, Gibson Clark. The building was designed by William R. Dubois.

Johnson School

712 House Avenue

Johnson School was constructed in 1923 and served as an elementary school until the late 1940s, when it became Johnson Junior High School.

The school was named for Edward Payson Johnson, a pioneer in the settlement of Cheyenne. Johnson came to Cheyenne in 1869 and was appointed U.S. district attorney for Wyoming in 1871. He also served in the Wyoming territorial legislature.

McCormick Junior High School

2001 Capitol Avenue and 6000 Education Drive

The original McCormick Junior High School, at 2001 Capitol Avenue, contained thirty-eight classrooms, a gymnasium, a library and an auditorium. The auditorium served as Cheyenne's Civic Center for many years before a new Civic Center was built.

Architects for this Collegiate Gothic–style school building, now a state office building, were William Dubois and Frederick Hutchinson Porter. A new McCormick Junior High School was constructed in north Cheyenne in 1975.

Carey Junior High School

1780 East Pershing Boulevard

The original Carey Junior High School was located at 1780 East Pershing Boulevard. It was constructed on the site of one of Cheyenne's three war worker camps.

A new Carey Junior High School was recently completed near East High School.

CHURCHES AND FRATERNAL ORGANIZATIONS

There are many churches throughout Cheyenne. Featured in this section are those institutions that were built in the early days of the settlement of Cheyenne and still exist within the historical downtown corridor of Cheyenne.

First United Methodist Church

108 East 18th Street

The First United Methodist Church was organized in Cheyenne in September 1867, a month before the Union Pacific tracks were laid into town. Two lots were purchased from the Union Pacific at the corner of 18th Street and Central Avenue in 1868. A small white frame building was erected at this site and was dedicated on September 28, 1870.

In 1890, construction began on the Gothic-style church built of red sandstone that stands at the same location today. The twenty-seven stained-glass windows were added in 1900. The building is in the National Register of Historic Places.

The church is famous for its luncheons available on parade days in July during the Cheyenne Frontier Days™ celebration. As early as 1890, the Methodist ladies were touted for providing interesting food to help raise funds for the church. In November 1890, the ladies held a "C" supper where all foods for the supper were to begin with the letter "C." A local newspaper said the fare was quite varied, with cold meat, chicken salad, clam chowder, celery, cake, coffee and cream.

St. Mark's Episcopal Church

1908 Central Avenue

The cornerstone for St. Mark's Church was laid on September 14, 1886. The Old English–style church was completed in May 1893. The building was constructed of Castle Rock stone. The tower of the church was constructed in 1924. A parish house was built in 1912.

During World War I, the parish house hosted dances for the soldiers stationed at Fort D.A. Russell. The dances cost ten cents, and the proceeds were used for improvements.

Many improvements have been made throughout the years, and the church is in the National Register of Historic Places.

St. Mary's Cathedral

2107 Capitol Avenue

The Gothic Revival–style church was built of sandstone quarried at Iron Mountain, north of Cheyenne. The cornerstone was laid on July 7, 1907, and the building was dedicated on January 31, 1909. The cathedral replaced the former Catholic church at 19th and Carey that had been dedicated in 1879.

The building was enlarged and renovated for the Diamond Jubilee celebration marking the seventy-fifth anniversary of the Cheyenne Diocese, February 21, 1962.

The tower on the southwest corner of the building is similar to St. Mary's in Winchester, England. The cathedral is in the National Register of Historic Places.

First Presbyterian Church

220 West 22nd Street

The cornerstone for the Gothic-style First Presbyterian Church was laid in 1923. The church, built of limestone with a lofty tower, was dedicated in March 1925. The church had been organized in Cheyenne in 1869 under the name of Krebs Memorial Presbyterian Church and met at a building at 18th Street and Carey Avenue.

Some of the stained-glass windows at the church are dedicated to the memory of members who perished in World War II.

Mount Sinai Jewish Synagogue

2610 Pioneer Avenue

Jewish settlers came to Cheyenne seeking religious freedom, and by 1888, there were enough Jewish families to incorporate Temple Emanuel. More immigrants began to arrive in Wyoming because of free land offered with the Homestead Act. Others arrived seeking more opportunities.

Mount Sinai was incorporated in 1910 in a small house on Eddie Street (now Pioneer Avenue). The cornerstone for the first Jewish synagogue was set on October 24, 1915, at that location on the corner of Pioneer Avenue and 20th Street.

The Jewish congregation moved to the new synagogue at 2610 Pioneer in 1950. The main sanctuary features several stained-glass windows. The largest window is twelve feet high and contains fifteen panes depicting a menorah. Other windows show highlights in biblical history and major Jewish holidays.

The dedication and groundbreaking ceremony for the Mount Sinai Jewish synagogue, October 24, 1915. *Wyoming State Archives, Department of State Parks and Cultural Resources.*

Saints Constantine and Helen Greek Orthodox Church

501 West 27th Street

Wyoming's first Greek Orthodox church was established in 1922 in Cheyenne and was consecrated in 1931.

Greeks have contributed abundantly to the culture of Cheyenne. They immigrated to Wyoming, where many worked in mines and for the railroad. When the Orthodox church was consecrated in 1931, the congregation was encouraged to be proudly Greek and American.

Cheyenne's Greek citizens strive to honor the past and build on the future. They are famous for sharing their hospitality and hosting the Annual Greek Festival held each fall.

The Masonic Temple

1820 Capitol Avenue

The Masonic order began in Cheyenne when Cheyenne Lodge Number One received its charter on October 7, 1868. The original temple was located on the north side of 16th Street between Pioneer and Carey Avenues.

The Saints Constantine and Helen Greek Orthodox Church around 1930. *J.E. Stimson Collection, Wyoming State Archives, Department of State Parks and Cultural Resources.*

The original Masonic Temple, built in 1901, on Capitol Avenue. *J.E. Stimson Collection, Wyoming State Archives, Department of State Parks and Cultural Resources.*

The cornerstone for the present Masonic temple was placed on June 6, 1901. A fire gutted the interior of the building in 1903, and it was completely rebuilt utilizing the shell that remained.

During the Spanish influenza pandemic that swept Cheyenne in the fall and winter of 1918–19, the temple was used as a temporary hospital to take care of the sick.

Much of the building remains unchanged from its original construction. It has a full gymnasium and elevated running track in the basement.

LIBRARIES

Carnegie Library

Capitol Avenue and 22nd Street

The Laramie County Library System was established in 1886 when Wyoming was a territory. Andrew Carnegie offered $50,000 toward a library building in 1899. The Carnegie Library opened on May 19, 1902, at Capitol Avenue and 22nd Street.

The first Cheyenne High School, *left*; the Carnegie Library, *center*; and St. Mary's Cathedral, *right*. Only St. Mary's Cathedral remains. *J.E. Stimson Collection, Wyoming State Archives, Department of State Parks and Cultural Resources.*

Laramie County Library

2800 Central Avenue and 2200 Pioneer Avenue

On October 19, 1969, a new library building was constructed and opened at 2800 Central Avenue. The historic Carnegie Library building reverted to the City of Cheyenne and was demolished in 1969. The county library on Central Avenue later became the Wyoming State Library.

A new three-story library building was constructed at 2200 Pioneer Avenue and dedicated on September 8, 2007. The building received an award as being the finest library of its kind in the United States upon completion. Affiliated branch libraries are located in Pine Bluffs and Burns.

HOSPITALS

Memorial Hospital of Laramie County/Cheyenne Regional Medical Center

300 East 23rd Street

Several tents and buildings preceded the construction of a substantial hospital at 300 East 23rd Street in Cheyenne. The hospital building was completed in 1883 on land donated by the Union Pacific Railroad.

Following a typhoid epidemic in the fall of 1900, the need for upgrades and repairs to the hospital was urgent. Funds for the project were unavailable, so women who had assisted in the typhoid emergency organized a group to help maintain and furnish the hospital. The Hospital Aid Society was formed to assist in aiding the remodeling of the hospital. The newly remodeled facility was called St. John's Hospital. The hospital also served as the center of the fight against the Spanish flu in 1918. The hospital was overwhelmed with patients and had to move some accommodations to the Masonic temple to cope with the epidemic.

A school of nursing was founded at the hospital in 1901, and six students graduated from the first class of St. John's School of Nursing in 1903. The school closed in 1933.

A two-story maternity ward was attached to the main building and completed in 1906. In 1911, the Union Pacific Railroad built a second two-story building that was connected to the main hospital and was to be used exclusively for the care of Union Pacific employees.

The hospital was officially named Memorial Hospital of Laramie County in 1919 after incorporation by Laramie County. In 1921, the original hospital was demolished, and a new building was erected. The name was changed

The Union Pacific Railroad Depot, built in 1887 in the Richardsonian Romanesque architectural style. *Photograph by Michael Dixon.*

The Deselms Art Gallery was formerly a hospital for Union Pacific employees in the late 1800s. *Photograph by Michael Dixon.*

Above: Under the Capitol dome, following the 2019 restoration. *Photograph by Michael Dixon.*

Left: Fireworks highlighted a celebration for the grand reopening of the historic Capitol on July 10, 2019. *Photograph by Michael Dixon.*

Above: The Historic Governor's Mansion, built in 1904. The nation's first woman governor, Nellie Tayloe Ross, lived in the mansion in the 1920s that today serves as a museum. *Photograph by Michael Dixon*.

Left: The Idelman Mansion, built in 1883, still stands across the street from the State Capitol. It is now part of the Capitol Square. *Photograph by Michael Dixon*.

Left: The Boyd Building, built in 1911, stood for many years as Cheyenne's tallest office building at the corner of Carey Avenue and 17th Street. *Photograph by Michael Dixon.*

Below: The Hynds Building, erected in 1922 of concrete and steel, replaced the Inter-Ocean Hotel that had been destroyed by fire in 1916. The building now houses art galleries and other small businesses. *Photograph by Michael Dixon.*

Right: The Majestic Building was designed by William Dubois and built by Francis E. Warren in 1907. It served as the First National Bank and today is home for several businesses. *Photograph by Michael Dixon.*

Below: The Gleason Building, built in 1913 by Francis E. Warren, has housed many Cheyenne business enterprises, including the Grier furniture company. *Photograph by Michael Dixon.*

The First United Methodist Church, built in 1890 of red sandstone in the Gothic style. *Photograph by Michael Dixon.*

The Presbyterian Church at 22nd and Carey Avenue. *Photograph by Michael Dixon.*

Above: St. Mark's Episcopal Church, built in 1886. *Photograph by Michael Dixon.*

Left: St. Mary's Cathedral was constructed in 1909 in the Gothic Revival style of sandstone quarried at Iron Mountain, north of Cheyenne. *Photograph by Michael Dixon.*

The Supreme Court Building, 1937, on Capitol Avenue was designed by Cheyenne architect William Dubois. *Photograph by Michael Dixon.*

The Becker Hotel was built close to the Union Pacific Depot in 1910 and often housed railroad employees. *Photograph by Michael Dixon.*

The City and County Building was built in 1917 in the Classical Revival style and designed by William Dubois. *Photograph by Michael Dixon.*

Many celebrities have stayed at the iconic Plains Hotel, erected in 1911 on the corner of Central Avenue and 16th Street. *Photograph by Michael Dixon.*

The Nettford Apartment building was constructed in 1911, reflecting the Greek Revival style. *Photograph by Michael Dixon.*

Samuel Corson arrived from Scotland in 1883 to build this Queen Anne–style home in the Rainsford Historic District using architect George Rainsford's signature fish scale shingles on the exterior. *Photograph by Michael Dixon.*

The Nagle-Warren Mansion was built in 1888 of stone rejected from the construction of the Capitol Building. It was covered with stucco in 1960 to protect the stone. It has operated as a bed-and-breakfast establishment for many years. *Photograph by Michael Dixon.*

The Whipple-Lacey Mansion, built in 1883, exhibits a combination of architectural styles. *Photograph by Michael Dixon.*

Top: The Phoenix Block was erected in 1882. It has housed various business enterprises, including a grocery store, a hotel and presently a western wear store. *Photograph by Michael Dixon.*

Bottom: A fine example of one of the remaining commercial Victorian-style buildings on 16th Street is the Commerce Building. *Photograph by Michael Dixon.*

The Atlas Theatre was originally built in 1888 to house offices and a tearoom. Cheyenne architect William Dubois designed the conversion to a theater in 1908. *Photograph by Michael Dixon.*

Holliday Park is the location of the historic Van Tassel Carriage Barn, built in 1886 and designed by architect George Rainsford. It is currently the home of the Cheyenne Artists Guild. *Photograph by Michael Dixon.*

Teepees are erected by various Native American groups each July at the Indian Village in Frontier Park during the annual celebration. *Photograph by Michael Dixon.*

The night show at Frontier Park attracts top performers and thousands of visitors each July. *Photograph by Michael Dixon.*

The Grand Entry Parade at Cheyenne has often featured a stagecoach. *Photograph by Christine Kronz.*

The Children's Village is located within the Cheyenne Botanic Gardens in Lions Park *Photograph by Michael Dixon.*

Above: Built in 1934, the Art Deco terra-cotta Airport Fountain was designed as a memorial to the early aviation history of Cheyenne. Also shown is the first airport terminal building. *Photograph by Michael Dixon.*

Left: The Cheyenne Depot Plaza hosts events throughout the year and serves as a present-day landmark in front of the historic Union Pacific Depot. Eight-foot-tall cowpoke boots, painted by local artists, are scattered throughout the city. *Photograph by Michael Dixon.*

Memorial Hospital of Laramie County around 1930. *J.E. Stimson Collection, Wyoming State Archives, Department of State Parks and Cultural Resources.*

to Frances Warren Pershing Memorial Hospital in memory of General John Pershing's wife, the daughter of F.E. Warren, who perished in a fire in San Francisco in 1915. The present core of Memorial Hospital is all that is left of the 1923 building.

Throughout the years, many improvements and additions have been added to the facility. These expansions were guided by Laramie County Hospital Foundation, which was established in 1978.

Throughout the years, the hospital was remodeled and expanded many times. One of the most significant changes was the construction of the West Tower Building, a seven-story wing attached to the main complex and completed in 1968. Many other major renovations have occurred, including expansion of the oncology facilities in the 1990s. Additional updates and expansions occur up to the present time.

Now known as Cheyenne Regional Medical Center, this facility offers care including pediatrics, family medicine and specialty care such as oncology, orthopedics and cardiology.

DePaul Hospital

2600 East 18th Street

DePaul Hospital was established in Cheyenne in the late 1940s and has served the community with a variety of services throughout the years.

Land for the building was donated by the Catholic Diocese of Wyoming and was managed by the Sisters of the Daughters of Charity for many years.

MUSEUMS

Cheyenne has many fine museums dedicated to the history of the city and the state of Wyoming. This section features museums in the downtown historical corridor of Cheyenne. Museums located in other areas of the city will be discussed in other sections of this book.

Wyoming State Museum

2301 Central Avenue

Established in 1895, the Wyoming State Museum exhibits and interprets the cultural heritage of Wyoming from prehistory to the present day. The museum's functions are guided by state statute to collect, preserve and interpret a diverse range of objects, including history, art, anthropology and natural history.

The museum's permanent exhibits trace Wyoming's past, featuring human history, major industries, paleontology, wildlife and landscapes. Temporary exhibits include a changing gallery that highlights different Wyoming artists.

The Cheyenne Frontier Days™ Old West Museum

4610 North Carey Avenue

Change and remembrance helped drive a new initiative for Cheyenne Frontier Days™ (CFD) by the mid-1970s. Faced with the continued decline of its old headquarters building, the CFD Committee opted to convert a corner of the Night Show Pavilion into its new home. Other portions of the building were converted into the business offices for racing and contestants. Spurred by the national bicentennial celebrations, it was decided to convert the rest of the building into a museum dedicated to the heritage of the American West and built around the extensive collection of parade carriages. From that time to now, the Cheyenne Frontier Days™ Old West Museum has grown to become a major attraction, keeping the excitement of CFD alive through the rest of the year and making significant contributions to collecting, preserving and sharing the legacy of Cheyenne Frontier Days™.

In 1956, the Cheyenne Frontier Days™ Committee had determined that the 1929 Dance Pavilion was in terrible condition and needed to be replaced. Realizing the growing potential for night show revenue, the committee determined that it would be a good idea to create a new Night Show Pavilion on land to the east of the arena. The new structure was to have a modern stage for musical entertainment; a large great hall for dancing, conferences and trade shows; and even a boxing arena. This area was to be screened off from a large concourse and concessions area that could be isolated from the hall, requiring patrons to pay to enter. To save money, the original iron trusses that supported the old pavilion roof would be reused over the great hall.

Opened in 1957, the new Night Show Pavilion served its purpose for the next twenty years and featured many well-known names in entertainment as well as political rallies attended by John F. Kennedy and Lyndon Johnson for the Democrats and an equal number of venues for the state's Republican Party. In the late 1960s, the night shows were moved to a mobile stage erected in the arena and the pavilion's usefulness declined. In 1975, the CFD Committee needed a new location for its headquarters and decided to occupy the southeast corner of the pavilion. The contestants' office and racing office were located on the west side of the building, but there was concern that the center portion, including the great hall, was underutilized.

Following the 1976 national bicentennial celebrations, the desire to preserve the history of Cheyenne Frontier Days™ and the need to protect the valuable parade carriage collection, it was determined that the center of the building would be best utilized as a museum. In late 1977, a large group of volunteers descended on the structure and began renovations. CFD contributed $100,000 for the project, and the museum opened its doors in 1978. Dedicated not only to the preservation of CFD history and its carriages, the Old West Museum sought to preserve and present the history of the American West and collected a large number of historic costumes and other items donated from around the country.

In 1981, a group of volunteers started the Western Art Show to benefit the museum. The new art show rapidly became one of the largest and most prestigious shows of its kind along the Rocky Mountain Front Range. As a result, the museum also began collecting significant pieces of western art to add to its permanent collection.

By the late 1980s, the museum had outgrown its original confines and built a major expansion, thanks to the generosity of James D. Vandewark, owner of Darigold Dairy. The expansion was completed in 1993, and renovations to the structure continued until 1996.

Since 2009, the mission of the Old West Museum has been to preserve and interpret the history of the "Daddy of 'Em All." From that time to now, the museum has grown to become a major attraction, keeping the excitement of CFD alive through the rest of the year and making significant contributions to collecting, preserving and sharing the legacy of Cheyenne Frontier Days™.

Cheyenne Depot Museum

121 West 15th Street

The Cheyenne Depot Museum is located inside the historic Union Pacific Railroad Depot. The museum was founded in 1993 to interpret Cheyenne's early history and that of the construction of the Union Pacific Railroad.

Earlier plans to create the Wyoming Transportation Museum were not realized. For several years, volunteers placed small exhibits at the depot and conducted tours.

The City of Cheyenne acquired the building from the Union Pacific Railroad in 2003. The structure needed several upgrades, including raising the west wing that had settled into an old buffalo wallow depression after the Cheyenne flood of 1985.

The Old West Museum was contracted to install the first exhibits detailing the city's rich railroad history, and the revitalized museum opened its doors in August 2004. The west observation and elevator complex was added in 2008 to give access to exhibits on the second floor.

Cowgirls of the West Museum

205 West 17th Street

The Cowgirls of the West Museum was founded in 1995 to honor women who contributed to western culture and history. In 2001, the Cowgirls of the West Museum and Gift Shop opened in downtown Cheyenne.

The organization is completely run by volunteers with the goal of presenting women's perspective on western history.

Nelson Museum of the West

1714 and 1717 Carey Avenue

The mission of the Nelson Museum of the West is to build an important collection of military, cowboy and Native American artifacts, western art and natural history material. The aim is to share this collection and educate people about the history of the Old West.

The museum was founded by Robert L. Nelson, who collected artifacts for many years before the original museum was opened in 1998.

On Memorial Day, May 31, 2021, the new Military Memorial Museum at 1717 Carey Avenue opened to the public. Nelson is proud to share his collection of thousands of artifacts from all branches of the military dating back as far as the Civil War and up to the present time.

Chapter 3

FARTHER AFIELD

AVIATION HISTORY

First Flights in Cheyenne

The story of Cheyenne's experience with aviation began shortly after the establishment of the city in 1867. The first known ascent of a balloon happened in Cheyenne on July 25, 1871. The ascent was part of the Lake's Hippo Olympian and Mammoth Circus, a widely popular show that was traveling the West on the newly completed transcontinental railroad.

For the next several decades, balloons made occasional appearances in the city. They were a curiosity for the people of Cheyenne and had no practical application beyond military observation and circuses.

Cheyenne citizens first heard about powered flight on December 18, 1903, when a small article in the newspaper announced the first flight of the Wright brothers. Little attention was paid, however, until the Wrights proved triumphant at the Paris Air Show in 1909. From then on, Cheyenne had a romance with the skies.

In early 1911, Cheyenne residents were interested in the efforts of resident Guy Stoddard to build an airplane in his yard. Stoddard was planning to launch his craft from the rodeo arena in Cheyenne. Crowds came to see the spectacle on March 14, but Stoddard was unable to get his plane off the ground. It was learned that the plane, which was assembled at the rodeo grounds on March 13, had been vandalized overnight. Even though

Stoddard planned to fix the plane and try again, he was unable to obtain the financial backing for the project and abandoned the plan.

By August 1911, two pilots had attempted to launch aircraft from the local rodeo grounds in Cheyenne. Charles Walsh and Harold Brinker both had airplanes they hoped to fly. In a spectacle to draw paying crowds, Walsh attempted to fly his Curtiss biplane on August 1. After several delays that included tearing down a fence surrounding the track, Walsh took to the air in front of a thinning crowd of disappointed spectators. He finally turned his plane toward the city rather than toward the crowd in the grandstand and was able to raise his craft approximately one hundred feet above the ground and disappear over the city and away from the spectators. It was reported he landed near a school, where crews hastily disassembled the craft and loaded it on a train to leave the city.

Harold Brinker had hoped to be the first man to fly in Cheyenne with his own Curtiss-type plane that he had built. His plane was seized by a gust of wind and smashed into the grandstands on July 27. Brinker eventually completed repairs on his aircraft and was finally able to get it in the air on August 15. He made continually higher and longer flights in and around Frontier Park and the city. By 1913, however, Brinker gave up flying and returned to his passion for auto racing.

Transcontinental Flight

Aviation greatness arrived in Cheyenne in 1919. It began in May with the arrival of the United States Army's Western Flying Circus. Several aircraft from the United States and its allies, as well as some captured German planes, were put on display and flew demonstrations as part of a Liberty War Bond Drive. Hailed as a success, it was the harbinger of things to come. In October, it was revealed that the army was to conduct the remarkable Transcontinental Air Reliability and Endurance Test, and Fort D.A Russell was to be a major airfield for the event.

The complicated test involved every type of aircraft currently in the United States Army inventory. Pilots would fly from both coasts to the opposite end of the country and back again. The first plane to complete the journey would be declared the winner. The army wanted to demonstrate that it was possible to defend the coasts of the nation by air. At the heart of this effort was General Billy Mitchell, who had spent time at Fort D.A. Russell as a signal corps officer in 1912. Cheyenne was considered an ideal location for the test for several reasons. The army base contained ground suitable for an airfield, and the location was at the lowest point that aircraft could cross the Continental Divide. The Union Pacific Railroad also provided an easily visible and unbroken landmark that pilots could follow across unfamiliar terrain, and the railroad could bring fuel and supplies for the venture.

Throughout October, citizens of Cheyenne saw history being made as several planes a day struggled through wintry skies and high winds. All planes had to stop at Cheyenne to report their progress. A few aircraft were damaged, and pilot Edward Wales lost his life near Elk Mountain in a crash early in the race. Eventually, pilot Belvin Maynard was declared the winner of the contest on October 18, 1919. In addition to military applications, postal officials hoped the race would help to establish the possibility of the post office operating a transcontinental airmail service.

Airmail

There were high hopes that the airfield at Fort Russell would become a natural stopping point for aviators who were expected to fly across the country in ever greater numbers. That hope seemed confirmed when the city was approached by the United States Postal Service in May 1920 to see if the community would be part of the world's first transcontinental airmail route, slated to get underway in early September. Both the city and the commanders of Fort D.A. Russell were excited by the prospect. Unfortunately, the War Department determined that the airfield at Fort Russell could not be used by civilian aviation. Undaunted by this news, the city quickly located property one mile north of the State Capitol to the east of Frontier Park suitable for the task.

On September 8, the first official flights of the transcontinental airmail route got underway. Buck Heffron was the first airmail pilot to leave Cheyenne early in the morning with westbound mail. The first eastbound mail arrived some hours later in a plane piloted by Jimmy Murray. From that day on, there have always been aircraft in Wyoming's skies.

The United States Air Mail Service employed about twenty maintenance men at its new facilities in Cheyenne. These men were responsible for keeping the six planes stationed here in excellent working order. To do so often required ingenuity and resourcefulness due to unexpected problems with the aircraft or a lack of parts. This innovation would serve these men well, as well as the pilots they worked with for many years.

The route the Cheyenne-based pilots flew was between Omaha and Salt Lake City. This placed Wyoming in the middle of their daily rounds. The challenge of the territory and its environment drew some of the finest pilots the airmail service could employ. Pilots like Hal Collison, Slim Lewis, Jimmy Murray, Frank Yager and others braved the wicked Wyoming winds, dense fog and sudden snow squalls and thunderstorms on a daily basis. Not every pilot was able to survive the experience. Johnny Woodward became the first airmail pilot at Cheyenne to be killed when he flew into a hill near Tie Siding south of Laramie in dense snowfall. Weather was bad, but so was the unreliability of the early aircraft in such harsh conditions. Many pilots, even the most skilled, found themselves temporarily stranded on mountaintops or in the wide-open spaces common along the route.

One pilot who was almost a victim of Wyoming's treacherous conditions in 1921 was Jack Knight. Blinded by snowfall while attempting to navigate Telephone Canyon on his way into the Laramie Valley, he flew into the ridge at the top of the canyon and was knocked unconscious. When he awoke, he was surrounded by the wreckage of his plane, his engine and hundreds of pounds of mail. With the aid of a local rancher, he found his way to medical treatment for a broken nose in Laramie and then headed back to Cheyenne. Once there, he secured another plane with another cargo of mail and finished his flight to Salt Lake City. This was only the beginning of Knight's legend. A few days later, on February 21, he helped complete the first night flight of the airmails across the continent in the face of stormy winter weather and a route he had never flown before. For a time, Jack Knight was the most famous pilot in America until overshadowed by Charles Lindbergh.

Heroics of pilots like Knight and the others kept the Air Mail Service operating day and night with a minimum of delay or loss, regardless of the weather. By 1924, the airfield at Cheyenne had electric lights to define its location and beacons that could be seen for up to fifty miles. To assist in daytime flying, several large yellow concrete arrows were placed on the ground, in the vicinity of the city, to help pilots find their way safely through the region.

Despite constant improvements and hard work by the crews and pilots, the United States Air Mail Service was in for difficult times. In November 1924, an accidental fire destroyed the first airmail hangar at Cheyenne. The calamity destroyed all the planes here, but no one was injured. Wyoming's Nellie Tayloe Ross, the first woman governor in the country, broke ground for four replacement hangars shortly thereafter, and operations continued. While there was no doubt as to the perseverance of the service, Congress

Pilot Jack Knight received minor injuries when he crashed his airmail plane on February 13, 1921. *Wyoming State Archives, Department of State Parks and Cultural Resources.*

Wyoming governor Nellie Tayloe Ross presided over a groundbreaking ceremony for new hangars at the Cheyenne Airfield in 1925. *Wyoming State Archives, Department of State Parks and Cultural Resources.*

was eager to divest itself of this costly and risky venture. In 1925, the Kelly Air Mail Act was passed. The intent was to remove direct involvement of the government in the transport of the airmail, instead giving it to commercial airlines. The catch was that these new companies also had to carry passengers.

Commercial Flight

In 1927, the Cheyenne division, part of Commercial Air Mail Route 18, was purchased by Bill Boeing, founder of Boeing Aircraft Corporation. This route covered the entire distance between Chicago and San Francisco. Creating a new airline for the job, Boeing Air Transport (BAT), Bill Boeing asked the airmail crews and the experienced pilots if they would consider working for his new company. The majority decided to do so, creating a veteran staff for the young airline. Boeing designed new aircraft with the latest instruments and aviation technology. The Boeing 40, his first airliner, was slightly larger than the airmail planes it replaced. The new aircraft had superior engines and flight characteristics. It also carried four passengers inside the fuselage behind the engine. The pilot, who sat behind them in an open cockpit, could offer no assistance to them in flight. While the pilots loved the new planes, a better solution for passengers had to be found. The solution was Boeing's first true airliner, the Boeing 80. This tri-engine biplane was luxuriously appointed. The pilot and copilot sat inside and could interact with the passengers. For the passengers, the added benefit of a bathroom was installed.

While this new aircraft was under development, the facilities at Cheyenne grew to meet the needs of Boeing Air Transport. A new administration building was constructed in 1929, followed by the largest hangar in the Rocky Mountain region. The old airmail hangars and facilities were likewise expanded and modernized. Cheyenne became the airline's center of operations with all administration, aircraft maintenance and pilot training happening here. Even the Boeing 80 was tested at Cheyenne to make sure it was up to the challenges of its environment.

Even with the most sophisticated and up-to-date amenities available to the needs of the flying public, BAT had difficulty convincing people it was safe to fly. Steve Stimpson, a ticket agent in San Francisco, found the solution. Why not have young female nurses serve as in-flight stewardesses to attend to the needs of the passengers? The company took a chance with the new concept and invited eight young women—including Ellen Church, Stimpson's inspiration for the new profession—to Cheyenne for training. Stimpson and Church created the blueprint for all future flight attendants in Cheyenne in May 1930. The eight original young women left Cheyenne in May to begin their jobs as the first women working in aviation. Their example transformed air travel around the world.

United Air Lines

By the end of 1930, Boeing Air Transport had combined forces with three other airlines to become United Air Lines. The new company moved its headquarters and stewardess training school to Chicago. The maintenance base for the expanded company remained in Cheyenne. All of the company's airliners, including the new Boeing 247, were maintained and modified with the latest technology here for service across the continent. It was here that the company installed the first de-icing equipment, the first geared propellers, the first variable pitch propellers and other innovations that later became standard in the industry. The workforce grew to five hundred personnel who worked in shifts around the clock to keep the company's planes in top condition. These craftsmen became so proficient that other airlines from across the country and around the world came to Cheyenne to witness their processes. Known as the "Roundhouse of the Air," the Cheyenne Maintenance Base was the largest facility of its kind in the country.

Several notable dignitaries visited Cheyenne because of its important location on the main transcontinental air route. Charles Lindbergh stopped in the city with the *Spirit of St. Louis* on his way west after his legendary transatlantic flight on September 2, 1927. Amelia Earhart came through Cheyenne on several occasions. Her first flight through Cheyenne occurred in 1928, when she was just passing through. In 1931, she stopped at Cheyenne in an autogiro as a promotion for Beech-Nut Gum and again in July 1932 when she took time to take in Frontier Days and crown Edith Gogerty our second Miss Frontier.

The Modification Center

The Second World War proved to be the zenith of Cheyenne's aviation might. Shortly after the attack on Pearl Harbor, United moved its pilot training facilities from the West Coast to Cheyenne to protect them from possible invasion. This school was soon moved to Denver, as the Cheyenne airfield became far too busy with a remarkable war production effort to allow for safe training space for the pilots. The incredible reputation of the United Maintenance Base made Cheyenne far more important for another reason. As the tempo of the conflict intensified, the U.S. Army Air Corps opened direct discussions with United Air Lines for some very special war contracts. The large, experienced staff proved to be a tremendous asset in the modification of the most powerful aircraft then in the United States inventory, the Boeing B-17 Flying Fortress.

A new facility, Modification Center No. 10, was built on the northeast corner of Cheyenne's Municipal Airfield. Two titanic 400-foot-long and 150-foot-wide hangars were constructed, along with other facilities.

At the outset, Boeing intended to fly hundreds of B-17s to Cheyenne as they were produced. These aircraft were "cookie-cutter" planes that were produced to a standard plan as fast as possible. The aircraft were transferred to Cheyenne, where the United Air Lines staff modified the planes to fly in any environment in the world, arctic, desert or jungle. The United crews also incorporated the latest innovations and defenses to the planes before sending them off to their theaters. The operation continued around the clock without stopping for the next three years. In addition to the Modification Center itself, massive new concrete runways were constructed that far exceeded the scale and scope of any that had come before. These served as the basis of the runways the airfield enjoys today, capable of handling almost any aircraft produced anywhere in the world.

While the Modification Center was in operation, housing in Cheyenne for the massive new workforce was a constant problem. To alleviate this situation, the War Department authorized the construction of three war worker camps of individual and family apartments. The first of these facilities was constructed in 1943 on the nearby grounds of the Frontier Days facility. This camp was followed by Careyville Acres and Van Tassell Terrace. The latter still survives nearly intact as the Pinewood Village Apartment complex in south Cheyenne.

On July 16, 1945, it was announced that production at the Modification Center would cease by the end of the month. Newer and more powerful bombers like the B-29 Superfortress were now filling the skies, and the B-17's day was coming to a close. From September 1942 to July 1945, Modification Center No. 10 produced 5,736 Flying Fortresses. These aircraft represented 46 percent of the type flown by the United States and its allies during the war.

United Air Lines soon began to ascertain the future of the airline. The future of the industry lay in four-engine aircraft, not the two that Cheyenne was optimized for. The demands of efficiency required the company to consolidate all of its maintenance activities and 2,600 staff in one location. The company knew that its needs for growth would far exceed Cheyenne's ability to either provide the new personnel or house them. In March 1945, United decided to move the maintenance base to San Francisco.

The Stewardess Training Center

Following the closure of much of its Cheyenne operations, United Air Lines recognized the value of the long-term relationship it had maintained with the City of Cheyenne and decided not to abandon it completely, offering to relocate its stewardess school to Cheyenne. The move coincided with the expansion of United's facilities in Chicago. The stewardess training center in Chicago had been demolished to provide space for more hangars, thus making it necessary to find new quarters for the school.

A portion of the Cheyenne modification center was repurposed for the stewardess training center. The upper level of a three-story brick building

An outside view of the United Air Lines Stewardess Training Center in Cheyenne in the 1950s. *Courtesy of Patricia Seibel Romeo.*

was converted into dormitories and training rooms for the students. A cafeteria was maintained in a separate building.

The United Air Lines Stewardess School operated in Cheyenne from 1947 to 1961, graduating more than six thousand women. With the arrival of the jet age, a new up-to-date school was constructed in Chicago. With the departure of the stewardess center, Cheyenne lost a profitable and popular aviation relationship with United that had existed for more than thirty years.

The National Guard

At another part of the airfield, a new chapter in Wyoming's aviation history began in 1946 with the founding of the Wyoming Air National Guard. Originally housed on the south side of Cheyenne's airfield, Wyoming's 187th Fighter Squadron received its contingent of P-51 Mustang aircraft after the U.S. Army's 402nd Fighter Squadron was deactivated. With United slowly reducing its footprint at the old Modification Center, the Wyoming Air National Guard moved into the third of the center's hangars in 1947.

The Wyoming Air National Guard (WANG) continued to evolve its operations at the airfield during this time as well. In 1956, it became the 187th Fighter Interceptor Squadron and was equipped with F-86J Sabre jets the next year. In 1961, commanders decided to change the mission of the WANG and converted to medical airlift operations as the 187th Aeromedical Transport Squadron, first flying the C-119 Flying Boxcar aircraft and then the graceful C-121 Super Constellations.

In 1966, the WANG became home to the 153rd Military Air Lift Group. It received its first C-130 Hercules aircraft in 1972 and has been flying versions of that storied aircraft from the Cheyenne airfield ever since. For a brief time between 1974 and 1975, the group was tasked with combat air transportation. Not all of its activities were for war. In 1975, the 153rd was selected to undertake new missions with the Modular Airborne Fire Fighting System. This system allowed them to convert the C-130 into an aerial fire bomber capable of dropping three thousand gallons of fire retardant onto a blaze. This capability remains a crucial part of the 153rd's mission to this day. In 1997, the 153rd flew 250 firefighting missions over the jungles of Indonesia, marking the first time that an American military aerial firefighting unit fought fires outside the continental United States.

After the attacks of September 11, 2001, the 153rd Airlift Wing became the first U.S. military unit to resume flying, delivering blood supplies around the western United States. In December 2001, five aircraft and their personnel flew to Oman in support of Operation Enduring Freedom, a mission that would take eight months. Flying in the Middle East and in Afghanistan, the 153rd received the Air Force Outstanding Unit Award with Valor. Deployed elsewhere in the world, the 153rd had an extended deployment during Operation Iraqi Freedom when two aircraft were dedicated to the effort in 2004–05. Deployments to Afghanistan were undertaken in 2006–07.

Today, the 153rd Airlift Wing provides crucial support for the nation's military efforts around the globe. Several deployments have been made to the Middle East, Africa, Central America and Asia with a total of twelve aircraft.

With the long and storied history of the Wyoming National Guard, a strong desire grew within the National Guard Association to preserve its heritage. In 1987, the Wyoming Militia Historical Society was founded with two goals: to write a definitive history of the Wyoming Guard and to establish a museum. Enthusiasm grew, and many items were collected. The adjutant general helped store the historical items in multiple locations for several years, but a location for a museum was still undetermined.

In the early 1990s, the old Cheyenne Armory on Pershing Boulevard became the repository for the numerous collections. With a storage site secured, the Wyoming Militia Historical Society volunteers actively promoted the history of the Wyoming Air and Army National Guard through programming, publication and exhibitions.

In 2007, the Cheyenne Armory was dedicated as the Wyoming National Guard Museum. Again, volunteers provided significant work in creating the museum's displays and organizing its expansive collections. In 2012, the Wyoming National Guard Museum became a sub-branch of the Wyoming Veterans Memorial Museum in Casper. Further renovations within the building continued until 2019, when the Wyoming legislature passed a bill formally establishing the museum. It is currently operated by the volunteers of the newly renamed Wyoming National Guard Historical Society and the Wyoming Military Department.

Cheyenne's First Airport Terminal

In 1927, the Boeing Aircraft Corporation started a new airline for Commercial Air Mail Route 18 between Chicago and San Francisco. This new airline, Boeing Air Transport, selected Cheyenne, Wyoming, as its headquarters due to its central location on the route. To house the operations of this new airline, a modern terminal building was constructed in 1929 and featured the best accommodations the airline could offer.

The new terminal was designed by the Austin Company of Seattle and Portland, Oregon, and built at a cost of $60,000. The building was constructed of brick and featured a lounge, coffee shop and restaurant for passengers; a locker room for pilots; and a sorting room for mail on the first floor. Incoming passengers entered from the north side, while outgoing passengers emplaned on the east side. The second floor of the terminal housed the offices for BAT operations on one side and traffic control on the other.

The hangar immediately to the north of the new headquarters was constructed as the largest hangar of its type in the Rocky Mountains. Here, all the maintenance on BAT's fleet of aircraft took place. It enclosed thirty-one thousand feet of space. Both buildings together cost $100,000. It was also in this building that Steve Stimpson, a BAT ticket agent from San Francisco, and Ellen Church, a graduate nurse who loved flying, implemented a plan to train eight young women to serve as the world's first stewardesses in the spring of 1930.

The Airport Fountain

The Airport Fountain built in 1930 near the entrance to Cheyenne's first and original airport terminal, on 8th Avenue. *Starley Talbott photograph.*

The United Air Lines Fountain, located at 8th Street and Warren Avenue, is one of the most widely recognized features of Cheyenne's original airport. Constructed in 1935 by the Denver Terra Cotta Company, it served as a memorial to the early pioneers of aviation.

This was a fitting location for the fountain, as the route through Cheyenne was the principal cross-country passenger route across America at that time. United Air Lines chose to construct the fountain in the popular Art Deco style and decorated with terra-cotta reliefs of the most advanced airplane then in its inventory, the Boeing 247-D. The Boeing 247 design held many firsts for the company. It was Boeing's first all-metal airplane, the first to be a monoplane and it heralded the arrival of the modern airliner. It was test flown over Cheyenne to ensure that the aircraft could handle operating at the high altitudes demanded as it passed through the Rocky Mountains.

The fountain has recently undergone major renovations and is now operable. Future improvements will serve to completely restore the fountain to its original appearance and condition.

Cheyenne's Second Airport Terminal

In 1957, the City of Cheyenne determined that it needed a new air terminal to reflect the up-to-date commercial and tourism opportunities in Cheyenne. The city engaged the Robert William Postin architectural firm, which submitted a variety of designs.

The original terminal concept was to have the structure clad in decorative brick screens and a flat roof to accommodate an outdoor dance floor and lounge. While this might have been a good idea during the summer months, it was obviously untenable for the rest of the year. Eventually, a design evolved that featured a fireproof building dominated by a sweeping space-age concrete roof that invoked the speed and grace of the jet age.

The new terminal featured an all-glass exterior on the front and a large interior waiting area for thirty passengers. Amenities included a restaurant and bar, a basement lounge, rental car offices and a gift shop for souvenirs and snacks. The structure opened in 1959 and served the community until 2018, when the current terminal opened.

One of the most widely regarded features of the 1959 terminal in later years was the Cloud 9 lounge located on the second floor. A popular evening destination, it was the favorite haunt of Governor Ed Herschler in the 1970s.

Eventually, security demands after the attacks on September 11, 2001, required a separate holding area to be placed in an area to the north of the terminal. This small new building was a double-wide trailer that continued to be used for passengers until the terminal closed.

Cheyenne's Third Airport Terminal

At the turn of the twenty-first century, the Cheyenne Airport Board began planning for a new terminal in 2007. It took a decade to raise the $18.5 million needed to build the new structure.

Built by Q&D Contractors to accommodate 250 passengers at a time—enough to fill three Boeing 737s—the new terminal was designed for simplicity to make travel comfortable and safe. Constructed out of materials that reflect the region's aesthetic, the terminal also includes murals and other artwork that help visitors and guests connect with Wyoming. Like its predecessors, the terminal has spaces for snack counters, restaurants and shops to meet the passengers' needs. Construction began in 2017 and was complete in 2019.

The architects intended the structure to reflect the sophistication of Wyoming's capital city and its location where the Great Plains and the Rocky Mountains meet.

F.E. WARREN AIR FORCE BASE

The evolution of a facility on the western edge of Cheyenne from a dusty frontier fort to one of the country's major U.S. Air Force bases is a story of epic proportions.

A Frontier Fort

On June 28, 1867, a combined expedition of surveyors and engineers from the Union Pacific Railroad Company and the United States Army left Julesburg, Colorado Territory, heading to a point at the base of the Rocky Mountains near Crow Creek. The destination was one that had been located four years earlier by the chief engineer of the Union Pacific, Grenville Dodge, as the point where the railroad would begin its climb over the Continental Divide. The army was interested in the area because the Union Pacific intended to construct major facilities to maintain its operations on the transcontinental railroad. Therefore, a fort would be needed to defend against possible attacks by Native Americans. The army also intended to create a significant depot for equipment repairs and supplies for the numerous forts that served the region.

On July 3, the Union Pacific party met a strong contingent of troops under the command of General Augur, then commander of the Division of the Platte. Augur and his troops participated in brief ceremonies commemorating Independence Day before heading north along Crow Creek, leaving behind Dodge and his survey party, who busied themselves with the plotting out of the new town of Cheyenne.

The army delegation selected a wide flat plateau three miles from the city to establish a fort to defend the new community. This post was named for Major David Allen Russell, who had died as a brevet general in the Second Battle of Winchester during the Civil War in 1863. The site was selected to be far enough outside Cheyenne in adherence to a law that no alcohol could be sold within a three-mile perimeter of a military post.

Once the site was determined, soldiers began constructing barracks for the enlisted men to be ready prior to the onset of winter. The original configuration of the fort centered on a diamond-shaped parade ground to include post headquarters, officers' quarters, a guardhouse and enlisted barracks. The post was further divided to support six companies of both cavalry and infantry. Buildings to the west were for the infantry and its officers, and the buildings to the east were for the cavalry. Farther beyond the parade field were the support buildings, including the bakery, surgeon's quarters, laundry, warehouses and workshops. Below the fort on the floodplain of Crow Creek were the stables for the horses, providing easy access to water. The first of the buildings to be complete were the barracks for the enlisted men. The officers and their families stayed in tents until their houses were

An aerial view of Fort D.A. Russell in the early 1900s. The diamond shape in the foreground is the original parade field. *Wyoming State Archives, Department of State Parks and Cultural Resources.*

complete the following year. During the harshest weather during the first winter, families were often taken to Cheyenne to find better shelter in frigid temperatures.

While Fort Russell was under construction, the Cheyenne Depot was also being built under the supervision of Colonel E.B. Carling between the fort and Cheyenne. This massive facility, more commonly known as Camp Carlin, was built by civilian contractors and soldiers, with most of the lumber coming from local suppliers. This facility proved to be of enormous importance because military supplies were transferred from that location by rail to be distributed to many forts up to five hundred miles distant.

Supplies left the Cheyenne Depot (Camp Carlin) by massive wagon trains guided by civilian teamsters. Forts that were supplied in Wyoming included Fort Bridger, Fort Fetterman, Fort Laramie, Fort Saunders and Fort Steele. The facility also served the important function of housing major repair shops for the maintenance of all types of military equipment, including vehicles and weapons. Camp Carlin continued operations until 1890 and employed up to 2,500 workers, many being extremely skilled craftsmen who lived both on the depot grounds as well as in Cheyenne. A similar number of mules, oxen and other animals were kept at the depot in support of their operations.

The numbers and types of troops stationed at Fort D.A. Russell were in constant flux due to the nature of the U.S. Army on the frontier during this time. Built after the Civil War, Fort Russell didn't demand constant numbers of troops to fight an established and determined enemy. Limited to a tiny number of soldiers, around sixteen thousand in all, the army had to not only man all of its garrisons throughout the West but also patrol the countryside to enforce the many treaties with local tribes in the region or to conduct punitive expeditions against interlopers or even open warfare against the Native Americans. The result often left Fort D.A. Russell with a token security force to protect government assets at the fort and the nearby depot.

While no battles were ever fought in the immediate vicinity of Fort D.A. Russell, its troops were often present at momentous occasions during the settlement of the region. The first significant involvement of its troops was in the escort of the 1867 Peace Commission sent to Fort Laramie to negotiate an end to Red Cloud's War, which had raged along the bloody Bozeman Trail since early 1866. Until peace was declared in late 1868, supplies for the forts along the trail were supplied from the Cheyenne Depot. In 1869, troops from Fort Russell joined a punitive expedition

Cavalry soldiers are shown riding across the parade ground at Fort D.A. Russell. *Wyoming State Archives, Department of State Parks and Cultural Resources.*

against the Cheyenne Indians in northwest Nebraska and again in 1873 along with troops from Fort Laramie.

In 1875, the United States government determined that the Sioux, Cheyenne and their allies must relocate to approved reservations, not only to maintain order but also to secure the use of the Black Hills for gold mining operations. In January 1876, an order was issued that all Indians must go to their reservations or be attacked. It is likely that few Indians in Nebraska, Wyoming or Montana received word of this order, yet the U.S. Army mobilized to enforce the edict. Troops from Fort Russell were deployed to assist in several attempts to drive the Native Americans to reservations in 1876.

The last engagement of troops from Fort D.A. Russell in the Indian Wars was in October 1879. Troops from the fort were sent to the White River Agency to deal with an uprising by the Ute tribe. On the route to their destination, the column stumbled upon a force of Ute warriors. Before a conference to negotiate was set up, someone opened fire, and a mêlée ensued in which several soldiers, including Major Thornberg, were killed. After the "Thornberg Massacre," further fighting was avoided, and the Utes were relocated to southern Colorado.

From that point on, the troops at Fort D.A. Russell were never again engaged in fighting to settle the frontier. Officers of the post continued to take their men out on patrol to protect the supply wagons and routes to the outlying forts. When back on the post, officers extended invitations to the community of Cheyenne to attend celebrations of national holidays, sporting events and weekly parade drills of the troops and performances by company bands.

In 1890, two momentous occasions occurred that changed the disposition of the fort: the United States Census Bureau declared the frontier closed, and Wyoming became a state. The need for the widespread forts in the area seemed to be past, and for the next several years, fort after fort in Wyoming and the surrounding states shut down. Fort Russell escaped the budget axe. Camp Carlin, the Cheyenne Depot, did not. New railroads such as the Fremont, Elkhorn and Missouri Valley; the Great Northwestern; and the Chicago, Burlington and Quincy made resupply from eastern points far more efficient. Many structures at the depot were sold off or torn down.

Relations between Fort Russell and Cheyenne remained mostly cordial. Occasionally, the soldiers of the fort were used to enforce the law in Cheyenne's early "Hell on Wheels" activities, or soldiers sometimes violated the laws and peace of the nearby community. One great example of cooperation was in 1897, when Captain Pitcher, in command of the fort while General Van Dorn was away on maneuvers, agreed to an appeal by the members of the Cheyenne Board of Trade to bring elements of the Eighth Infantry to participate in a new celebration of Cheyenne's frontier past on September 23. Without seeking approval of the War Department, Pitcher eagerly contributed to the inaugural celebration. Troops under his command participated in pitching tents, military style, near the fairgrounds at Pioneer Park, doing drill demonstrations and participating in a sham battle to the thrill of the audience. This was the first engagement of the United States military with Cheyenne Frontier Days™, and the relationship has continued unbroken through today.

A More Permanent Fort

It was also during the interlude between the Indian Wars and the twentieth century that the fort began to expand. Permanent brick structures and new waterworks facilities began to be constructed on the post. Prior to these more substantial structures, a series of fires had burned down several

The original officers' row at Fort D.A. Russell, around 1868. These wooden structures were replaced with brick ones. *Wyoming State Archives, Department of State Parks and Cultural Resources.*

structures on the fort. Several buildings that were destroyed were not replaced. Fire remained the greatest threat to the fort well into the early years of the next century.

Before that century dawned, there was one additional conflict that Fort Russell became involved in. With the outbreak of the Spanish-American War, the relatively quiet Fort D.A. Russell became a hub of activity for the training of Wyoming volunteers desiring to aid in the war effort. Foote's Infantry, Torry's Rough Riders and the Alger Light Artillery all trained briefly at the post prior to their departure to Florida and California for an assault on the Philippines. After that archipelago fell under the control of the United States, a long insurrection began in 1899 that drew more soldiers to the islands to keep order.

The Bells of Balangiga were captured and put on display at Fort Warren. They were returned to the Philippines in 2018. *Wyoming State Archives, Department of State Parks and Cultural Resources.*

One element, Company C of the Ninth Infantry, was detached from Fort D.A. Russell for service on the island of Samar in August 1901. After an initial period of cordial relations between the troops and the people of Balangiga, a local seat of government, relations soured, and on September 28, insurrectionists and their local supporters launched a carefully coordinated surprise attack on the Americans, killing half of them. After the initial shock, the American troops rallied and took the town with assistance from an armed steamship and reinforcements from Company G of the Ninth Infantry. Two bells and an antique Spanish cannon were seized from Balangiga and taken to Fort D.A. Russell, where they were displayed as war trophies until the bells were returned in 2018.

World War I

By the outbreak of World War I, Fort D.A. Russell had grown to a regimental post hosting five thousand personnel and their families. Infantry and cavalry were supplemented with the addition of artillery units, and the Pole Mountain

Military Reserve was established between Cheyenne and Laramie for large-scale field exercises. With its many new and impressive brick structures and its significance at the center of the nation and on the national transportation routes, the fort had become an important facility. After the United States entered the war, thirteen artillery units were trained at the fort before being sent to Europe. There was no small matter of pride felt by the fort and the community of Cheyenne that one of the officers who had served at Fort Russell, General John J. "Blackjack" Pershing, was the commander-in-chief of the American Expeditionary Force.

The most pressing threat to the safety of the fort during this conflict was the outbreak of the Spanish flu in October 1918. Several soldiers became sick with the influenza, and many died. Health officials on the fort and in Cheyenne were wary of visitors during this time, and both remained relatively isolated from each other for a brief period of three months until early February 1919. By that time, Fort Russell had been designated as one of the principal discharge facilities for soldiers returning from the war. Many thousands of soldiers coming home to Wyoming, Colorado, Nebraska and other states came to the fort before making their journey home.

In May 1919, a unique war bond drive came to the fort in hopes of spurring the people of Cheyenne and the local community to buy more bonds to help pay the massive debt incurred by the war. On May 1, Major Tooey Spaatz arrived with several Allied and captured German warplanes to put on a flying circus demonstration for the citizens of Cheyenne. The officers of Fort Russell quickly prepared an airfield south of Randall Avenue next to the railroad tracks so that the aircraft could be offloaded, assembled and then flown. It was a remarkable demonstration that excited the imaginations of soldiers and civilians alike and served as the harbinger of things to come.

A Transcontinental Race

In September 1919, Fort Russell was selected by General Billy Mitchell, himself a one-time soldier at the post, to be one of the principal stops on a massive demonstration of air power. The Transcontinental Air Reliability and Endurance Test was an unprecedented event in aviation history. The participating aircraft and their crews had to fly across the continent to the opposite coast and back again. Mitchell, a fanatical believer in the value of air power, sought to remove all doubt in the minds of those in Congress as to the possibility of defending the nation by air from attack.

Fort D.A. Russell was a perfect location for a major stop on the race route. Its location placed it close to the Union Pacific Railroad, which doubled as a means of resupply for the aircraft and a handy landmark inexperienced pilots could follow between Chicago and San Francisco. It was also near the easiest crossing of the Continental Divide and passage through the Rocky Mountains. With the help of local organizations from Cheyenne, fort officers and men cleared a suitable landing area north of Randall Avenue. Fuel oil reserves and electric lights for night landings were set up, and a canteen was established for pilots and their crews, all of whom were required to stop at the fort during the race.

The first aircraft arrived from San Francisco on October 9. Unfortunately, bad weather hampered flights and cost one pilot his life. Captain Edwin Wales died when he struck a mountain while trying to fly through unfamiliar terrain near Elk Mountain. The landing field at Fort Russell was named Wales Field in honor of the fallen pilot. There were several more non-fatal crashes during the race before Lieutenant Belvin Maynard claimed victory on October 18.

The Airmail

In the spring of 1920, news arrived at the fort that the United States Postal Service intended to establish a major division point at Wales Field for the proposed Transcontinental Air Mail Route then being developed. Wales Field was a natural choice for a landing site, but the secretary of war determined that the facility needed to remain dedicated to military use in case of national emergencies.

As a result, a new airfield was established north of Cheyenne for the purpose. This airfield became the Cheyenne Municipal Airport. The airmail service was successful, followed by the establishment of Boeing Air Transport and the Cheyenne Modification Center during World War II. Wales Field faded into insignificance, and as a result, the modern-day F.E. Warren Air Force Base is the only such facility without its own landing strip.

Target and Maneuver Reservation

For the rest of the 1920s, Fort Russell became an important training center for artillery, antiaircraft machine gun, cavalry and infantry divisions that rotated through the post on a relatively regular basis.

The attraction of the fort for training lay with the extensive three-thousand-acre Target and Maneuver Reservation thirty miles west of the post near Pole Mountain. During this time, polo became a very popular sport at the fort, and it was the site of several major competitions between army and civilian teams. Summer camps were held for area cadets and Reserve Officer Training Corps units from regional universities and high schools.

Fort Francis E. Warren

In 1930, President Herbert Hoover changed the fort's name to honor Francis E. Warren, who had recently died in Washington, D.C. Wyoming's first governor and a longtime senator, Warren was a Congressional Medal of Honor winner for his bravery at the Battle of Port Hudson during the Civil War. He had also been a longtime supporter of the fort and its garrisons. During his interment ceremony, two thousand soldiers marched in his procession, and artillery fired a final salute.

With the onset and through the course of the Great Depression, Fort Warren remained remarkably stable. The First and Twentieth Infantry Regiments were permanently stationed at the fort, as were elements of the Seventy-Sixth Field Artillery. Little improvement on the post took place, with the exception of the construction of a football field between the fort and Cheyenne, south of Randall Avenue, as military budgets were severely constrained. This situation began to change in 1935 as war clouds darkened the horizon in Asia and Europe and money began to flow into the military to make preparations.

World War II

With the outbreak of the Second World War in 1939, the United States implemented major efforts in preparation for possible participation in the conflict. Starting in mid-1940, National Guard and Reserve units were activated. Congress also implemented the Selective Service Act, bringing

Members of the Ninth Cavalry Band, an all-Black unit commonly known as a buffalo soldier unit, were stationed at Fort Warren from 1911 to 1912. *Wyoming State Archives, Department of State Parks and Cultural Resources.*

thousands of young men into the army through the draft. In September, Fort Warren was designated as a major training center for these new soldiers. By the spring of 1941, several thousand new recruits had arrived at the fort to begin training as "replacements." Hundreds of new temporary buildings were constructed on the fort, primarily in the river bottoms below the original fort along Crow Creek. The fort grew at a breathtaking pace and by 1942 could accommodate twenty thousand soldiers, with a peak of twenty-six thousand for a brief time.

After the attack on Pearl Harbor and America's official entry into the war, the new facilities fell under the command of the Quartermaster Corps. Soldiers who came were to receive not only basic training but also in specialized tasks as motor pool technicians, truck drivers, cooks, field hospital personnel and numerous other occupations. Units of the Women's Army Auxiliary Corps also began training at Fort Warren in 1943.

From 1943 until the end of the war, Black soldiers began training at Fort Warren almost exclusively as, even during this great national crisis, segregation in the military continued to be the standard. Alongside these men were units of the railroad battalions of the Transportation Corps. These units were being trained to operate locomotives in the newly liberated areas of Western Europe for the Allies and were able to take advantage of the extensive rail facilities at Cheyenne for their preparation. However, Black soldiers had been stationed at the base occasionally throughout the years.

Toward the end of the war, hundreds of captured enemy soldiers were kept at the fort. The prisoners were mainly Germans who had been captured in North Africa. There were Italians present too, but they were considered guests at this juncture due to Italy's quitting the Axis Powers and now fighting on the side of the United States.

Francis E. Warren Air Force Base

With the conclusion of World War II, Fort Warren's training focus continued at a reduced pace. The post became a deactivation center for the region, and hundreds of returning troops were discharged to civilian life here. The Germans and Italians were sent home by 1946, and fort personnel were reduced to a minimum. The National Security Act of 1947 created the United States Air Force, and despite its lack of an airfield, the new service took possession of Fort Warren in June 1948.

Now known as Francis E. Warren Air Force Base, the post became home to the 3450th Technical Training Wing. Charged with training airmen to support the massively expanding U.S. Air Force, the base returned to the role that it had served for the army's Quartermaster Corps with greater emphasis on administration, motor pool, equipment and facilities maintenance, as well as the inclusion of a fixed-wire communications school.

After a brief three-month interlude where the airmen of the base helped dig Wyoming out after the powerful blizzard of 1949, operations at the base continued to grow. Warren Air Force Base became a significant facility for the Air Training Command during the Korean War. The base grew to house twelve thousand personnel and their families. To accommodate so many people, five hundred housing units were constructed on the former site of Wales Field. The base operations and the huge number of people on the base made the facility the single greatest economic engine for the community of Cheyenne, an important distinction it retains to this day.

The training role of Warren Air Force Base did not diminish after the Korean War thanks to the steady and increasing demands for highly trained personnel during the Cold War with the Soviet Union. This conflict took a major turn when the Soviets revealed their capacity to launch a payload into orbit with Sputnik. Realizing the ease with which a nuclear warhead could be substituted for a satellite, the United States immediately ramped up its own capacity to do the same. Fears were confirmed when the Soviets revealed the world's first intercontinental ballistic missiles during a parade in Red Square that same year, and a new arms race was launched. By November 1957, it was announced that F.E. Warren Air Force Base would become home for America's new Atlas missiles, with launch sites being built throughout the countryside surrounding the base and Cheyenne. In 1958, training duties were slowly transferred to other bases, and the Air Training Command turned over the base to the Strategic Air Command. The first unit to arrive for this new role was the 706th Strategic Missile Wing. As the transition happened, the number of airmen and officers on the base

The front gate at F.E. Warren Air Force Base around 1950. *Wyoming State Archives, Department of State Parks and Cultural Resources.*

was reduced to a sustainable level of thirty-five hundred personnel. Brick buildings for the new role of the base were constructed, and the now idle temporary structures built in the prelude to World War II were dismantled and removed. The base, now home to the Thirteenth Strategic Missile Division, soon began the work of installing the new weapons.

The first missile site for F.E. Warren Air Force Base was site A, constructed twenty-one miles northwest of Cheyenne. Three other missile facilities designated B, C and D were constructed off U.S. Highway 85 northeast of Cheyenne, south of U.S. 30 between Cheyenne and Burns to the southeast and near Granite Canyon to the southwest. By the end of 1961, twenty-four missile launch facilities were active in Wyoming and northern Colorado.

For the first time in its history, the base became isolated from Cheyenne out of necessity. A high chain-link fence was installed around the post for security purposes, and people coming on base had to be cleared for access. This unfortunate, but necessary, change in the relationship between Cheyenne and the base was offset to a great degree with the release of the old Target and Maneuver Reservation to civilian recreational use.

In 1961, it was announced that a new missile, the Minuteman 1, was becoming operational. Unlike the Atlas missile, which needed to be fueled before launch, the new weapon utilized a solid-fuel booster that could be kept in an inert and ready state until the moment it was needed. The superior potential of this combat system to be ready in an instant meant that the old Atlas was obsolete. Warren AFB was designated as one of the principal launch sites for the new missile.

For the next several years, new silos were installed in Wyoming, Nebraska and Colorado for two hundred Minutemen. These new hardened silos were widely dispersed over hundreds of square miles. Activated in 1963, these new weapons were under the control of the Ninetieth Missile Wing and lived up to their potential as a rapid and reliable nuclear deterrent force. By 1965, the old Atlas missiles were deactivated in favor of their new replacements. With the dispersed locations of the many missile silos under the base's control, it was deemed necessary to activate a UH-1 helicopter unit to ferry maintenance and security forces over the vast missile fields of the region. These aircraft continue to fly in Cheyenne's skies performing this duty well into the twenty-first century.

As the Cold War continued unabated and even intensified in the 1980s, a controversial new nuclear weapon system, the MX missile, came out of development and was deployed to Warren Air Force Base. The LG-118A, or "Peacekeeper," was a monstrous weapon containing ten independently targeted warheads that were far more lethal and accurate than the Minuteman III. Fifty of these weapons were housed in specialized solos north of Cheyenne beginning in December 1986. The new weapons sparked a highly intensified nuclear arms race between the United States and the Soviet Union. Many historians have expressed that this increased strain on the Soviet system helped lead to several summits at the end of the 1980s to end the Cold War and the eventual dissolution of the USSR.

In 2002, U.S. president George W. Bush and Russian president Vladimir Putin signed the Moscow Treaty, which was intended to reduce the number of nuclear weapons in each country's arsenals by two-thirds. As part of this agreement, the fifty Peacekeeper weapons were dismantled, with the final Peacekeeper missile being deactivated with a ceremony on September 20, 2005. To commemorate this momentous time in Cold War history, the Quebec 01 Missile Alert Facility, once the showcase facility within the Peacekeeper system, was restored as a museum and opened to the public in August 2019.

Francis E. Warren Air Force Base remains an important component of the nation's nuclear deterrent shield. The base thrives as its own community near Cheyenne meeting the myriad needs of its military members and the multitude of veterans who have made Cheyenne their home. The post continues to adapt and grow to meet the nation's evolving defense needs and will soon undergo major upgrades with the replacement of the aging Minuteman III with the new Ground-Based Strategic Deterrent system. Installation of the new missiles is scheduled to begin prior to 2023 and will be a tremendous boost to the capabilities of the base as well as to the Cheyenne community.

In 2021, the F.E. Warren Air Force Base Air Park opened. The park was created so that visitors may park near the base's central gate west on Pershing Boulevard and take a short walk to view the three decommissioned intercontinental ballistic missiles displayed there. Also on display is a Bell UH-1F Huey helicopter, which was used to transport military personnel to and from the base from 1966 to 1980. The new park offers visitors and residents a view of the history of the base without having to gain access to the base itself.

For the foreseeable future, Cheyenne and the air force base will continue to be the close neighbors they have been since the beginning.

CHEYENNE FRONTIER DAYS™

A Cowboy Sports Show

Cheyenne Frontier Days™ started as an effort to boost passenger ticket sales for the Union Pacific Railroad and the flagging Cheyenne economy. The concept was the brainchild of Union Pacific Railroad ticket agent Frederick Angier. In the mid-1890s, Angier tried to encourage the people of Denver to purchase day-trip tickets on the UPRR. The whole nation was in the grip of an economic depression, and the railroad was struggling to get by. He struck upon the concept of encouraging nearby outlying communities to have a fair based on something unique to their economy. For several communities, this meant celebrating their main crop. Loveland honored Corn Day, and Greeley celebrated Potato Day.

When Angier arrived in Cheyenne to promote such a celebration, the members of the newly formed Cheyenne Board of Trade could not think of anything that Cheyenne raised, except for "a little hell from time to time." Stymied for a solution, Angier was struck by a scene while waiting for a train to Denver. He spied a group of cowboys wrestling an unruly horse onto a boxcar. The contest was by no means decided, and a crowd had gathered to cheer as much for the horse as for the men. A delighted Angier cancelled his trip and sought out E.A. Slack, the son of Esther Hobart Morris and editor of the *Cheyenne Daily Leader*. The two men formulated a new concept to have cowboy sports as the center of a fair.

The board members, along with Angier, fleshed out a more detailed plan. Not only would they celebrate cowboy sports, but they would also celebrate the wild frontier experience of the community. The board organized a list of responsibilities for its members to develop and promote the idea. The old Wyoming Territorial Fairgrounds west of the city were perfect for a sports extravaganza. Ranchers around the area were intrigued by the idea of a contest and were willing to lend their toughest animals and their cowboys to the event. Officers at Fort D.A. Russell were also asked to attend, bringing troops to demonstrate their important connection to the city and their skills at warfighting. Native Americans were asked to share their mysterious yet colorful culture and traditions with visitors. There were many other additions to be added, and local businessmen were asked to contribute to covering the expenses. The Union Pacific promised special rates for passengers to Cheyenne from Denver and all points east and west, as well as advertising at all their depots.

A panoramic photo of the frontier rodeo held at Pioneer Park in 1902. *J.E. Stimson Collection, Wyoming State Archives, Department of State Parks and Cultural Resources.*

In less than thirty days from Angier's first meeting with the board, Cheyenne's first Frontier Day was held on September 23. From all accounts, the celebration was a tremendous success. More than four thousand people crammed into the tiny stands at the fairgrounds to see horse races, bucking and pitching contests, Native American dancers and military drills. The event impressed the guests, and word spread. The reputation of this seminal celebration was so significant that not only was there a demand for a second performance the following year, but Buffalo Bill Cody contacted the board of trade and offered to have his show coincide with the fair to draw even greater attention.

Buffalo Bill Performs in Cheyenne

With the second Frontier Day, the pattern for success was set. The Buffalo Bill show brought hundreds of riders from around the world, a mock stagecoach robbery, large troupes of Native American dancers and spectacular demonstrations of shooting and riding skills in addition to the home-grown excitement of local cowboys competing against tough animals in authentic ranch sports. Despite very cold and bitter weather, twenty thousand people attended the show.

The Cheyenne show's ability to experience such tremendous and instant appeal needs to be explained. Buffalo Bill Cody was a big contributor to the show's initial success, even if indirectly. For decades, the expansion into the American frontier had fascinated the people of the East and around the world. The tales of man against nature, man against man and man against beast were plentiful at every turn. Multiple dime novels promising fantasies of adventure and danger to the readers in the rapidly industrializing East were eagerly consumed. Buffalo Bill himself capitalized on this appetite by promoting his own experiences as a Pony Express rider, buffalo hunter, army scout and friend to the Indian. His shows were already in great demand not only in America but also in Europe.

Smaller shows had tried to imitate Cody's success, but Cheyenne had a unique opportunity. Cheyenne's remarkable frontier beginnings, including its "Hell on Wheels" days and its glory as the capital of the cattle barons, had

Native Americans have long shared their Native dances and traditional dress while performing at Frontier Park. *J.E. Stimson Collection, Wyoming State Archives, Department of State Parks and Cultural Resources.*

already left an indelible mark on the minds of people already predisposed to the thrill of the frontier. Aided by the popularity of Owen Wister's novel *The Virginian* that crystalized the cowboy as a mythic western hero, Cheyenne's show was primed for greatness.

For their part, Native Americans were pleased to participate in events like Buffalo Bill's Wild West Show and Cheyenne's show because it allowed them to escape the restrictive environment of their reservations. These shows also encouraged the preservation and sharing of traditional ceremonies, dances, dress and language that were actively suppressed at home. Americans were fascinated with the first peoples of the nation and were willing to travel great distances to see them.

The Greatest Western Celebration

The success of Cheyenne Frontier Days™ continued its meteoric rise through the 1900s. Billed as the greatest western celebration in the country, it had no peers. Cowboys came from around the nation to compete. To win a contest at Cheyenne was to earn the victor the title of world's champion. Not content to rest on its laurels, CFD continued to adapt and try new contests to elicit even greater enthusiasm.

Beginning in 1898, cowgirls were encouraged to demonstrate their mettle in massive horse races. These women soon began to challenge the men to bust the meanest bucking broncos.

In 1904, Black cowboy Bill Pickett of the 101 Ranch of Oklahoma startled the crowd by "bulldogging" a steer. The crowd was amazed as the man leapt from his horse onto the horns of a rushing steer. Pickett wrestled the animal to a stop and then subdued it by biting the animal on its lower lip. Stunning demonstrations of skill were supplemented with demonstrations of unique shooting skills, trick riding and even riding wild buffalo in front of the crowds.

Chief among the performers and stock contractors that helped the new event grow was the remarkable Irwin family. C.B. Irwin, a local rancher, was the biggest booster of the celebration. His family cooked for and cared for the traveling cowboys, provided the toughest stock and provided the cowboy stars and exhibition talent for the show. The Irwin daughters were all renowned racers who dominated the ladies' relay race for years. The family could be counted on to be a big part of the drama until C.B.'s death in 1934.

C.B. Irwin played a crucial role in the success of Cheyenne Frontier Days™. *Wyoming State Archives, Department of State Parks and Cultural Resources.*

One of Irwin's greatest contributions to the rodeo was the introduction of the legendary bucking bronco Steamboat. This docile horse became ferocious in the arena and a renowned "bucker" that threw most men who dared ride him. He got his name from the noise he made when he bucked. As a colt, an accident broke his nose, and cowboys removed a piece of bone to help him heal. Thereafter, every time he snorted, he sounded like the whistle of a riverboat, giving him his name and his appeal. Throwing rider after rider, the horse continued to draw crowds even after he was eventually ridden. He was the first animal superstar of rodeo, and he cut his teeth at Cheyenne.

The Irwins were only one of the families who got involved with the event and stayed involved. Other families included the Hirsigs, the Merritts and the McInerneys, but they are by no means the only folks from Cheyenne and the surrounding communities who have helped the show thrive even to this day.

President Roosevelt Visits Cheyenne

In 1903, CFD was paid the great honor of being visited by the president of the United States, Teddy Roosevelt. Roosevelt, himself a consummate cowboy, loved the event. The people of Wyoming gave him a horse and a saddle as a parting gift. Roosevelt promised to return and did so again in 1910.

With the president's visit, the star for Cheyenne Frontier Days™ was ascendant. Recognized as the premier western sports event in the nation, it became the draw from around the West and beyond.

The New Frontier Park

By 1907, the festival had outgrown its original home in the Wyoming Territorial Fairgrounds, and a new location was needed. Located about a mile north of its original location, the new Frontier Park was dedicated to the west of a series of reservoirs established for the railroad. Some of the original stands were taken down at the old location and erected at the new site. A new iron grandstand was also built, as was significant bench seating for the ever-growing crowds.

The 1908 celebration was the first to take place at CFD's current home. As usual, large crowds were on hand. Again, the dazzling performances of cowboys—including Dick Stanley, who rode Steamboat to a standstill—along with racers, trick riders and other spectacles, enthralled the crowd. Three paniolos (cowboys from Hawaii) came to Cheyenne to try their hand at the world's championship of steer roping. No one knew what to expect from these men who had traveled the farthest anyone had yet come to participate in the event. Ikua Purdy, already a legend on the islands, won the contest with remarkable skill. He became the first world's champion who wasn't from Wyoming. To this day, his victory at Cheyenne is celebrated on Hawaii.

While Wyoming lost the crown for the first time, this only lent to its mystique. By the time of Roosevelt's return, the clamor from people around the nation and across the globe to see what Cheyenne had to offer had grown. The event was filmed by the Tournament Film Company in 1910 and 1911, and this footage was shown in several theaters worldwide. By this time, several other communities across the West had decided that if Cheyenne could profit from a great celebration of western culture, they could too. In quick succession, Cheyenne was joined by Pendleton, Oregon; Calgary, Alberta; Houston, Texas; San Francisco, California; and other major cities that hosted their own rodeos. Modeled after Cheyenne's great event, each of these new rodeos adopted the "Cheyenne Rules," and the sport of modern rodeo was born.

In 1911, CFD had another first added to its already stellar reputation: it became Wyoming's first airfield. A carpenter by the name of Guy Stoddard had built a plane in his front yard that spring. Enthralled, the local papers enlisted the aid of the general committee to give the young man a place to demonstrate his aircraft. The committee agreed, and Stoddard's plane was intended to lift off into the heavens in front of a crowd sitting in CFD's grandstands. Unfortunately, things didn't go as planned, and Stoddard's contraption never took off. Later that year, local racecar driver Harold Brinker built his own plane on the CFD grounds with the committee's blessing. Unfortunately, strong winds damaged his plane, and it was left to a traveling aerial stuntman, Charles Walsh, to be the first to fly over Cheyenne. He, too, flew from the arena and would be the last to do so.

Airplanes were not the only new mode of transportation bringing people to CFD. As early as 1906, automobiles began to make their appearance during the celebration. At first, they were a curiosity. Soon, they became the preferred method of getting to the show, especially after

Steer ropers Archie Kaaua (*left*), Jack Low (*center*) and Ikua Purdy (*right*) from Hawaii participated in the rodeo in 1908. Purdy won the steer roping event. *Wyoming State Archives, Department of State Parks and Cultural Resources.*

the establishment of the Lincoln Highway in 1913. From that time to the early 1940s, automobiles raced on CFD's track, both as part of the show and as part of a growing racing circuit.

World War I

The entry of the United States into World War I in 1917 was a frightening time, even for CFD. Fearing that all of the cowboys would be drafted and the show would have to be cancelled, the community was relieved when the demand for men wasn't as high as was expected. Cowboys still came, and the show kept going.

In May 1918, a special edition of Cheyenne Frontier Days™ was held for a contingent of Belgian soldiers who stopped in the city on their way back to the Western Front. They had originally fought alongside the Russians on the Eastern Front. When that country fell out of the war in 1917, the United States arranged for them to cross the Pacific and North America on the Union Pacific Railroad. It was one of the oddest CFDs ever held, but the Belgian troops were grateful for the hospitality.

Cowgirls and Hollywood Stars

The 1920s were the heyday of the cowgirl at CFD. Women like Prairie Rose Henderson, Mabel Strickland, Fox Hastings, Lorena Trickey and many others brought a touch of glamour to the show, along with some great performances.

Hollywood was also deeply interested in Cheyenne's rodeo, with several western stars, including William S. Hart and Tim McCoy, becoming regular patrons. Other stars like Douglas Fairbanks also came to the show, as did journalists, artists and many local and national politicians.

The Pageant of Transportation

Even though parades had been part of the celebration for years, in 1925, a new parade format was introduced. With a little creativity and a large number of unused carriages sitting in Cheyenne's carriage houses, the new format was created.

Dozens of old horse-drawn vehicles—including the original Cheyenne to Deadwood stagecoaches, Conestoga wagons, ambulances, hearses and many other vehicles—were featured in the parade, called the Pageant of Transportation. By 1927, the format had become a regular feature at Cheyenne Frontier Days™ with a cast of hundreds of men, women and children, all dressed in period clothing. Bands from around the nation, Native Americans, soldiers, cowboys and celebrities waved to the crowds, who eagerly waved back.

A New Rodeo Innovation

In 1928, a new innovation was introduced into the CFD arena that would revolutionize the sport of rodeo. In its earliest days, riders had to wait until a team of cowboys subdued a horse, saddled it and let the rider attempt to get on before their ride could begin. This was later modified with a front entry chute that allowed horses to be saddled one at a time and then released.

The new system, the side entry chute, met with skepticism from cowboys. Eight animals at a time entered a long chute. As they reached the end, a small gate would slide closed behind them, allowing the animals to be kept separate and saddled independently. Once the animal was ready, the side of the chute would open, and each animal needed to do a quarter turn before it could exit and begin the ride. Cowboys came to appreciate the new arrangement, and the rodeo became faster and more entertaining as a result. This side chute system is now the standard for every rodeo in the world.

Miss Frontier, the Night Show and HEELS

In hopes of bringing new crowds and more prosperity, following the advent of the Depression, Jean Nimmo was crowned as the first Miss Frontier in 1931. As the show's official ambassador, Nimmo was a constant presence, greeting the crowds with a smiling face. The role of Miss Frontier and her lady in waiting continues as these young women charm would-be visitors as they travel the country visiting other rodeos and communities to boost CFD.

However, even with the aid of these lovely women and a surprise visit by Amelia Earhart, the general committee realized that the event wasn't making enough money to cover its expenses. Every effort was made to cut costs, even reducing the show by a day. The chamber of commerce, the

Pilot Amelia Earhart was a guest at Cheyenne Frontier Days™ in 1932. She is shown with Miss Frontier Edith Gogerty, William Hass (*far left*) and E.T. Storey (*far right*). *Wyoming State Archives, Department of State Parks and Cultural Resources.*

parent organization of CFD, issued bonds, hoping that local businesses would help underwrite the show. As a result, the generosity of local banks, the community and cowboys who were willing to ride for smaller purses saved the show from being cancelled. By 1933, even more financial support cleared the show of debt, and it became profitable again. This was the closest the show had ever come to being shut down for its first 123 years.

The year 1935 was another remarkable time of change. Great cowboys like Turk Greenough were a new generation of contestants. Bull riding and bareback bronc riding made their first appearance as official contests.

Night shows were added to the entertainment. Sally Rand, the celebrated nude fan dancer, became the hit of the night show after some considerable misgivings. A delightful guest to the end, Rand also spurred the concept of the white buckskin dress as the official uniform of Miss Frontier.

Another landmark change happened in 1935 when Ed Storey, a former chairman, mused to a group of fellow volunteers that they were being poorly treated by the general committee even though they were donating their time and talent to the show. The men agreed and decided to form an association representing men, and later women, who gave freely of themselves for the perpetuation of the event. The group was forever after known as the HEELS, a name coined by the members to refer to themselves as "we're a bunch of heels for doing this for free." The organizers spelled the name with capital letters, but it is not an acronym. This association has provided the bedrock of a massive volunteer community that continues to support the show and keep expenses down, to the envy of all other rodeos and many other large events.

World War II

While Cheyenne Frontier Days™ weathered the blows of the Depression well through the rest of the decade, times again became uncertain with the onset of World War II. Realizing that the nation was in its most desperate hour, the committee inquired of the War Department if the event should be cancelled, as resources spent on the celebration would be better spent for the war effort. The War Department concluded that the continuation of the celebration was one of the bright spots on the homefront and a happy occurrence that would be a balm to the soldiers and workers.

Encouraged, CFD continued through the war without hesitation. With many young cowboys drafted into the service, their place was taken by soldiers from nearby Fort Warren, who put up a good show for their fellow troops. Even Turk Greenough was given temporary leave of his duties to perform at CFD. Visitors were scarce during the war, but those who did come were shown all the hospitality the town could muster.

The crews of the Memphis Belle B-17 bomber were beneficiaries of this welcome when they toured the country in 1943. At the conclusion of the war, Frontier Days settled into a period of steady growth and popularity.

Change and Growth

Aided by westerns in film and the new wonder of television, Cheyenne's event drew many thousands of people from around the country annually. The stars settled on Cheyenne during this time as a constellation of Hollywood and television actors descended on the city for the rodeo.

The *Denver Post* ladies' relay race, a regular event since 1906, was discontinued in 1946.

The beloved chuck wagon races were introduced in 1952, and the chuck wagon pancake breakfast appeared on Cheyenne's downtown streets for the first time in 1953. In 1954, the United States Air Force thrilled thousands with the first ever public performance of the famed Thunderbirds precision flight team.

Some down-to-earth changes also took place on the CFD grounds. In 1957, a new Night Show Pavilion was constructed on the easternmost end of the park, and the Indian Village, which had moved around the grounds from year to year, finally settled on the corner of 8th Street and Carey Avenue. The reality of the various tribes not being able to produce enough costumes for the event led the committee to purchase a lot of authentic regalia for the dancers and create several lodges for their stay on the grounds.

In the early 1960s, the CFD Committee began to look at the event as a business and not an adjunct to the chamber of commerce. The business acumen of the committee had manifested itself in considerable profits. After considerable debate and some acrimony, the CFD Committee was able to keep all the profits that the show generated for its next budget. By controlling its own funds, the group began to plan for its own future. While the chamber and CFD continued to cooperate through the next decades, the chamber relinquished its role in the celebration in 1990, and CFD incorporated in 1992.

The 1960s also saw a move into the big-time night show business. While evening entertainment had always been a significant part of the celebration, it was decided to book top acts. A transportable stage was built so it could be pulled in front of the grandstands, and the pursuit of talent was launched. *Gunsmoke* stars Doc and Festus were the first big headliners, followed by others like Michael Landon and Loren Green of *Bonanza*.

Larger and more glamorous night shows offered "star power" entertainment. With the addition of such performers, an expanded B stand on the arena's west side in 1971 made it possible for more fans to attend. Roy Rogers with Dale Evans performed, as did Jerry Reed and Larry McNeely from the *Glenn Campbell Show*. The best and brightest stars in entertainment have regularly appeared ever since. Examples include Johnny Cash, Roy Clark, Barbara Mandrell, Tanya Tucker, Mel Tillis, George Strait, Garth Brooks, Reba McIntyre, KISS, Willie Nelson, Charlie Daniels, the Oak Ridge Boys, Randy Travis, the Judds, Post Malone, Taylor Swift and Chris LeDoux.

In 1970, cowgirls returned to the arena after nearly three decades of absence. The Dandies, a dedicated group of teenage female riders, performed dazzling displays of horsemanship and precision maneuvers. These young women have also served as ambassadors to other rodeos, and their skills have met wide acclaim across the country. The next year, barrel racing emerged with a flourish and secured a place for women once again among the pantheon of annual champions.

Any discussion about Cheyenne Frontier Days™ would be incomplete without mention of the magnificent cowboys and cowgirls who compete in the rodeo. Because of its heritage and prestige, CFD has been the one rodeo that all professional rodeo contestants dream of winning, and no pedigree is complete without a CFD buckle. The constellation of cowboy stars that descend on the rodeo every year is too numerous to mention all by name, but a few demand attention: Kristie Peterson, Billy Etbauer, Trevor Brazile, Ty Murray, Harrison Halligan, Ralph Buell, Chris LeDoux, Charles "Sharkey"

Lane Frost completed a ride on a Brahma bull on July 30, 1989, but was injured during the ride and perished in the rodeo arena in Cheyenne. He is honored at Frontier Park with a monumental statue by artist Chris Navarro. *Courtesy of Wagner Perspective, from the Old West Museum.*

Irwin, Ikua Purdy, Bill Linderman, Fred Whitfield, Ike Rude, Lane Frost, Tuff Hedeman, Larry Mahan, Jim Shoulders, Turk Greenough, Casey Tibbs and Mabel Strickland.

These names and others burn bright in the CFD Hall of Fame, and they are joined every year by others who compete and win their glory here.

The Tradition Continues

By the 1980s, Cheyenne Frontier Days™ was as successful as ever, spurred on by the recent "urban cowboy" craze sweeping Hollywood. Even so, the rodeo stumbled onto hard economic times after it ran into financial difficulties due to its massive constructions of B stands and its new Exhibition Hall. Volunteers again came to the rescue by helping to produce a good show while keeping costs low. In 1984, the group began to cultivate major sponsors, many of whom were eager to give their support to the rodeo and help the organization climb its way back to profitability. The facilities were expanded with the building of a new East Stand in 1993.

In 1996, CFD celebrated its 100th consecutive show. It had endured the many wars, depressions and economic downturns of the twentieth century and was poised to enter the twenty-first in grand style. The numbers of patrons continued to climb through the 1990s, and the night shows became the major extravaganza of the event. The profits for the night shows showed such considerable potential that they began to impact every other aspect of the rodeo. As a result, time schedules were changed for parades and pancake breakfasts, and even the rodeo itself had to take on a reduced time in order to ensure that preparations were made for the massive concerts to follow. The result sped up the rodeo, making it even faster-paced and more exciting.

After the turn of the millennium, Cheyenne Frontier Days™ thrived. In the early 2000s, a new attraction in the form of the Wild Horse Gulch was created on the east side of the arena to draw visitors and shoppers into that previously unused part of the park, and it proved a great link between the CFD entrances, the Indian Village and the Old West Museum. By 2018, annual ticket sales reached almost a quarter of a million visitors. Bucyed by its increasing success, CFD constructed another longtime dream, an official CFD Headquarters and event center, in 2019. This glamorous structure houses the offices for the corporation as well as special event halls for the volunteers and special VIP guests of the rodeo. Situated at the

The Cheyenne Frontier Days™ parade winds its way from the Capitol to the historic Union Pacific Railroad Depot. *Courtesy of Wagner Perspective, from the Old West Museum.*

southwest end of the arena, it now stands as a testament of the celebration's expansive legacy and bright future.

That future took a brief hiatus in 2020 when the COVID-19 epidemic brought the amazing event to a stop. Not wanting to expose the many contestants, patrons and volunteers to the risk of the disease, it was decided by the CFD Committee and health officials that the celebration would not be held until the following year. Fortunately, by the summer of 2021, the strong national effort to combat the epidemic was taking effect, and CFD was authorized to carry on. With the 125th celebration having welcomed visitors once again to the greatest western show, the organization and its fans look forward to its limitless horizons.

LARAMIE COUNTY COMMUNITY COLLEGE

Laramie County Community College (LCCC) has been an important part of Cheyenne's educational community for decades, offering two-year programs designed to prepare students for transition to university life, a career within the trades and ongoing training and proficiency education for the local workforce. In addition, the campus has offered many opportunities for life enrichment, early childhood development and diverse cultural opportunities for Cheyenne.

Established in 1968, the foundation of the college followed a dedicated movement to create an institution for post-secondary instruction and technical training. Approved by Laramie County voters on May 21 of that year, a board was created to secure operational funding, land and scholarships with the objective of opening the college by September 1969.

Land for the college was donated by the Arp and Hammond Hardware Company and Herbert Reed on the extreme southeastern corner of the city. Construction began on three buildings for administration, classes and student services in mid-1969. In the meantime, temporary administrative offices were established at 609 West 29th Street, with the first classes in basic adult-level education held at the Westside Neighborhood Youth Center.

When the completion of the buildings on campus was delayed, registration and classes were held in the First Methodist Church. Classes were also held at St. Mark's Episcopal Church and the First Presbyterian Church. Even with this dispersed beginning, the first semester saw the enrollment of 1,217 students across nineteen academic and vocational offerings, suddenly making LCCC the second-largest of the seven community colleges in Wyoming.

Laramie County Community College. *Starley Talbott photograph.*

The new buildings were completed in November 1969, and all of the LCCC operations commenced. The first three structures currently serve as the Administration Building, the Center for Conferences and Institutes and the Training Center. These humble beginnings provided the seed for a rapidly expanding campus that filled the needs for a similarly expanding clientele.

Expanded Facilities

In August 1971, a bond issue allowed for the construction of a science building (now the Education and Enrichment Center), finished in that year, and two other edifices for Business and General Studies (now the Andrikopoulous Business and Technology Center), the Auto Diesel Center (now focused solely on automobiles), Physical Education (now part of the Recreation and Athletic Complex) and an Instructional Resource Center (now the Ludden Library and College Community Center). The original

Agricultural Building, which is now the Auto Body Building, followed. All of these structures were constructed of prefabricated concrete walls, and most were connected by long corridors allowing students to move from building to building out of the wind, if not in heated comfort.

In 1975, the college achieved a milestone when it was awarded accredited status by the North Central Association of Colleges and Secondary Schools. By that time, the campus served 3,076 students.

In 1977, LCCC took over the licensed practical nursing program that was originally part of the curriculum for Albany County School District No. 1.

In 1979, a $6.8 million bond issue allowed for further expansion of the college with modern environmental systems on the campus. The construction of the Arp, Fine Arts, Student Services (now the Crossroads Building), the detached Construction Trades and Plant Maintenance Buildings and a large multipurpose room to the Physical Education Building were completed by 1981. A new Arena and Agricultural Building was constructed in 1985.

In 1990, a large bond issue passed that allowed the college to construct a new science building. The nursing program had expanded, as had the need for a new oral hygiene program.

Sports Programs

The Laramie County Community College Golden Eagles sports teams began shortly after the campus opened in 1972. Initially composed of teams in men's and women's basketball, volleyball and golf, the program was dismantled after 1992 due to budget cuts. The college's rodeo team escaped dissolution and continued to represent LCCC through the rest of the decade and beyond.

In 2002, the Golden Eagles returned with both men's and women's soccer and men's basketball and volleyball as part of the National Junior College Athletics Association. In 2016, women's basketball was reinstated and has provided dominant seasons for several years in Region IX. LCCC currently holds nineteen conference titles, with the majority of eleven titles held by the women's soccer team. The men's soccer team also has a considerable record with five wins. The men's basketball team and volleyball team have each earned a title one time.

The Twenty-First Century

In the twenty-first century, Laramie County Community College continued to expand, adding multiple new structures and services. In 2016, the campus added a state-of-the art Flex Tech Building to house its diesel mechanics and welding programs.

In 2017, the Clay Pathfinder Building was completed, housing the campus student services, science classrooms and a floor for the University of Wyoming.

In 2021, the residence halls at LCCC finished a major expansion, providing housing for 632 students. There was also a significant expansion of the Fine Arts Building with the addition of the Surbrugg Prentiss Auditorium, providing four hundred seats for musical and theatrical productions.

The campus sits on 271 acres with twenty-five buildings, but this is not the end of its facilities. The Albany County Campus, composed of a single structure, was added in Laramie in 2006 to extend LCCC's services into that county.

At present, Laramie County Community College offers forty-nine academic programs in eight pathways dedicated to agriculture, the arts,

The Clay Pathfinder Building at Laramie County Community College. *Starley Talbott photograph.*

public service, science and engineering, business, health science, information technology and the trades. It also provides ongoing adult education, workforce development, life enrichment, young and high school programs and cultural events.

Laramie County Community College reached a peak enrollment of 6,367 students in the 2011–12 academic year and constantly adapts to the demands of local businesses, students and the community at large. It has proven to be an excellent source of knowledge and community enrichment that contributes dramatically to the quality of life in southeast Wyoming.

PARKS AND RECREATION

Parks

Cheyenne today has many attractive parks scattered throughout the city and among the many different neighborhoods. Citizens may enjoy activities including walking, biking, picnicking and playing games such as baseball, softball, soccer, tennis, golf and many other activities.

Baseball was played in Cheyenne as early as 1867, when Fort D.A. Russell had a team. By 1910, a semi-professional team called the Cheyenne Indians was formed. They played in the "Little World Series" in Denver in 1923. Today, dozens of baseball and softball teams play on Cheyenne's many diamonds.

The Union Pacific Railroad donated the land for the first city park in 1867. The park was located south of the State Capitol between Capitol and Warren Avenues and 22nd and 24th Streets. The park was treeless for a number of years until Arbor Day on May 6, 1882. A water system was established for the area, and hundreds of trees were planted. Today, the park has been replaced by the Supreme Court Building and the Barrett Building.

The year 2021 is the thirtieth anniversary of the Cheyenne Greenway, a much-beloved amenity for Cheyenne's citizens. Nearly forty-five miles of paved non-motorized trail wind through many of Cheyenne's neighborhoods and parks.

Cheyenne's most well-known parks include Lions Park, Holliday Park, Pioneer Park, Frontier Park and American Legion Park. In 1975, the city gave the American Legion Park to the State of Wyoming for the second Governor's Mansion.

Sunbathers and swimmers enjoy a day at Sloans Lake in Lions Park. *Wyoming State Archives, Department of State Parks and Cultural Resources.*

Lions Park

Carey Avenue and 8th Street

Lions Park is popular, with Sloans Lake being the centerpiece of the park. A grand opening of the park was held in 1880 to celebrate the driving park by the lake.

There are many picnic areas, walking paths and shelters within the park. Many activities are available, including swimming, fishing, boating, skating, tennis and other games.

The Lions Club, in cooperation with the City of Cheyenne, has worked to beautify the park and provided funding for plants and landscaping.

At various times, there have been amenities in the park, including a kiddie land and miniature train ride, which no longer exist. In the 1930s, the Works Progress Administration installed a sunken garden that existed at the present site of the park's outdoor performance pavilion.

The Kiwanis Community House provides a venue for many activities. The Cheyenne Municipal Swimming Facility was built in 1976. Bicycle and walking routes wind throughout the park. Located within Lions Park are the Botanic Gardens and Paul Smith Children's Village.

Botanic Gardens

The Cheyenne Botanic Gardens was founded in 1986, based on an earlier project, the Cheyenne Community Solar Greenhouse. The Botanic Gardens' purpose is to cultivate growth and enrichment in the community of Cheyenne by providing a treasured garden space for enjoyment, celebration and education. The gardens include nine acres of perennial and annual landscapes. There is also a collection of specialty exhibits and a year-round vegetable garden.

The centerpiece of the gardens is the Shane Smith Grand Conservatory, opened in 2017, featuring a lush, tropical plant collection.

Located within the gardens is the Paul Smith Children's Village. The site includes a preexisting stone building and stone walls surrounding a courtyard that once was a parks maintenance garage. It was constructed in the 1930s as part of the Works Progress Administration. The site was converted to the Children's Village in 2009 and named for Paul Smith, a longtime enthusiast and supporter of the Botanic Gardens.

Holliday Park

Morrie Avenue and 17th Street

Holliday Park provides many attractions for Cheyenne citizens. It is well known and recognized as the location of one of the "Big Boy" steam train engines that once traveled the rails from Cheyenne. Engine Number 4004 is the largest coal-fired steam locomotive in the world. It was built in 1941, retired in 1962 and restored in 2018.

Minnehaha Lake provides enjoyment for park visitors. On Arbor Day in 1897, schoolchildren planted trees along the lake shore. The park originally featured punting canals and separate islands joined by decorative bridges.

The Cheyenne Artists Guild's home at Holliday Park is located in the former Van Tassell Carriage Barn. The barn was built in 1886 and designed by architect George Rainsford. It was moved from its former location to Holliday Park.

Another interesting building at Holliday Park is the Warren Rest House. It was designed in 1902 by prolific Cheyenne architect William Dubois. The first governor of Wyoming, Francis E. Warren, donated funds for the structure in 1902 in memory of his wife, Helen. It was originally located in the park where the Wyoming Supreme Court Building stands today. It was restored in 2018 during the restoration of the Wyoming State Capitol.

The Warren Rest House, a structure to honor Helen Warren, the wife of Francis E. Warren, once stood at the City Park south of the State Capitol. It was later moved to Holliday Park and was restored in 2019. *J.E. Stimson Collection, Wyoming State Archives, Department of State Parks and Cultural Resources.*

Pioneer Park

Pioneer Park is one of the oldest parks in Cheyenne and was the location of the first Frontier Days rodeo in September 1897. Early fairs were held at the park, where folks entered their food and needlework for exhibit. Livestock were also exhibited at the fairs. At the first Frontier celebration in 1897, approximately four thousand spectators filled the grounds and crowded into the grandstands to watch the rodeo.

Other activities at the park have included bicycle races and horse racing. There have also been other sports played at the park, including baseball and football.

Frontier Park

Carey Avenue and 8th Street

Frontier Park is discussed in the section about Cheyenne Frontier Days™.

Recreation

Cheyenne supports a wide variety of activities for recreational opportunities. One early popular place was the Lawn and Tennis Club, which no longer exists. It was much like the present-day country club, where members could play tennis or other games. Many private parties were also hosted at the club.

Cheyenne today has many public and private recreational facilities. Activities include golf, tennis, baseball, softball, basketball, football, soccer, hockey, bowling, swimming and other recreational opportunities.

MEMORIALS AND CEMETERIES

City of Cheyenne Cemetery

2501 Seymour Avenue

The City of Cheyenne maintains the grounds at the cemetery complex north and south of Pershing Boulevard, with the cemetery office located on Seymour Avenue. The cemetery complex is bordered on the north by the Cheyenne Airport; on the east by Morrie Avenue; on the west by Seymour Avenue; and on the south by 23rd Street.

Within the city cemetery are several areas established by different groups of citizens. They include Lakeview, Olivet, Odd Fellows, Jewish and Beth El.

Lakeview Cemetery is the oldest of the segments within the City of Cheyenne Cemetery. The first recorded burial there was in May 1875. Lakeview Cemetery contains monuments to many of the area's earliest residents. Each monument has a story connected to the person or family buried there. These monuments serve as a repository of the city's history and a reflection of the growth and development of Cheyenne, Wyoming and the West.

Olivet Catholic Cemetery was approved in 1887. In the 1920s, improvements including the iron fence and the entrance gate on Pershing Boulevard were completed. In 1923, a granite Celtic cross was placed at the Priest's Circle portion of the cemetery.

To the west of Olivet Cemetery is the Odd Fellows Cemetery, established in 1888. It was operated by Cheyenne Lodge No. 1 of the IOOF until 1959, when the deeded land was returned to the city. Only IOOF members may be buried there.

Between the Odd Fellows Cemetery on the south and Beth El Cemetery on the north lies Mount Sinai Jewish Cemetery, established in 1888. The Jewish and Catholic cemeteries are owned by the Jewish Cemetery Association and St. Mary's Catholic Church, respectively. However, the grounds are maintained by the City of Cheyenne.

Beth El Cemetery, west of Olivet Cemetery and north of the Jewish cemetery, was created by the city council in the mid-1920s. The first recorded burial in Beth El was on November 19, 1925. Beth El Cemetery includes sections purchased specifically for Spanish-American War veterans, veterans of foreign wars, members of the American Legion and Greek Americans.

Other cemeteries located in the vicinity of Cheyenne include Mountain View Memorial Park, Cheyenne Memorial Gardens, F.E. Warren Air Force Base Cemetery and the National Cemetery.

Two Graves at Lakeview Remind Us of Life's Tragedies

The monument to Willie Nickell tells the story of a young boy who was murdered at this ranch north of Cheyenne in 1901. This story relates back to the saga of Tom Horn. Horn was accused of the murder, allegedly confessed to it and was hanged for the offense. A plaque on the north side of the monument briefly explains the story. The east side of the monument lists the names of Willie's parents, Kels and Mary Nickell.

Within the tract dedicated to the Warren family stands another grave marker telling about a tragedy for a young family. The Warrens were prominent in Cheyenne, and Francis E. Warren served as territorial governor, state governor and United States senator. His daughter, Frances Helen Warren, was married to Captain John Pershing in 1905. The couple had four children and lived in many places around the world where Pershing, who had been promoted to general, was stationed. Frances and their three daughters, Helen, Ann and Mary, died in a fire at the Presidio in San Francisco in 1915. They are buried in the Warren family plot at Lakeview Cemetery.

STATUES AND FOUNTAINS

Robert Burns Statue

There are several memorial statues located throughout Cheyenne. One of these is the Robert Burns statue at the corner of 26th Street, Randall Avenue and Pioneer Avenue. The statue was donated by Mary Gilchrist to the City

Left: A monument honoring fourteen-year-old Willie Nickell stands at Lakeview Cemetery. *Starley Talbott photograph.*

Below: In the Warren family plot at Lakewood Cemetery is the grave of Frances Warren Pershing and her three daughters, who perished in a fire at the Presidio in San Francisco in 1915. *Starley Talbott photograph.*

of Cheyenne in 1928. Mary Gilchrist, a native of Scotland, was one of the leaders of the Robert Burns Society in Cheyenne.

Buffalo Soldier Statue

Randall Avenue and 32nd Street

In a small triangular-shaped park at Randall Avenue and 32nd Street is a statue paying tribute to a buffalo soldier. The first Black soldiers stationed at Fort D.A. Russell (now F.E. Warren Air Force Base) were from Troop K of the Ninth Cavalry in 1887.

Native Americans in the Southwest had begun calling Black soldiers of the Ninth and Tenth Cavalry by the title of "buffalo soldiers." The name came from the belief that the hair of a Black soldier looked like the dense and curly hair of a buffalo. The buffalo was also deemed to be sacred to the Native Americans for its strength and courage.

According to legend, in 1867, Private John Randall, Troop G, Tenth Cavalry, fought against seventy Cheyenne warriors by himself at a location in the Southwest until help arrived. Randall was said to have been armed only with a pistol and to have fought like a cornered buffalo. Thus, Randall earned the name of a "buffalo soldier." The term spread quickly to include all Black soldiers in the United States Army.

Additional troops of buffalo soldiers were posted at Fort D.A. Russell in the ensuing years. Four companies of the Black Twenty-Fourth Infantry were posted at the fort in 1898. Troop E of the Nineteenth Cavalry was stationed at the fort in 1902. The Ninth Cavalry arrived at the fort in 1909, where it remained for a year and was named the championship baseball team at Fort D.A. Russell in 1912.

Most of the Black soldiers throughout the nation were stationed stateside and served in peace. However, there was segregation and racial strife. Incidents involving violence against Black members of the military occurred in several locations in the United States.

From 1943 until the end of World War II, Black soldiers began training at Fort Warren almost exclusively as, even during this great national crisis, segregation in the military continued to be the standard.

When the Black soldiers of Troop E of the Tenth Cavalry were at the fort in 1902, they participated in Cheyenne Frontier Days™. According to news reports of the time, the soldiers were well received by the people of Cheyenne.

As a testament to the strength and courage of Black soldiers, the statue on Randall Avenue in Cheyenne salutes these brave men.

A statue honoring the buffalo soldier stands in a small park near 32nd Street and Randall Avenue. *Starley Talbott photograph.*

National Humane Alliance Fountain

A portion of a historic fountain now resides at Lakeview Cemetery. How it ended up there and its original purpose and location are an interesting bit of Cheyenne history. The National Humane Alliance presented the fountain to Cheyenne in 1908 for the purpose of providing a watering place for animals.

The National Humane Alliance was founded in 1897 by Hermon Lee Ensign, a philanthropist and animal welfare advocate. He contributed a large amount of money toward building and donating animal drinking fountains for any city that requested one. Cheyenne was one of the more than one hundred cities that obtained one of the unique granite structures that were built in Maine.

The *Cheyenne Daily Leader* reported on the dedication of the fountain in its May 23, 1908 edition. Abbie Brooks, the daughter of Wyoming governor Bryant Brooks, turned on the water to the fountain. Other dignitaries gave speeches, and students performed songs.

The fountain was located near the Union Pacific Railroad Depot in the middle of the intersection at Ferguson (later named Carey) and 15th Streets. It was about six and a half feet tall and consisted of a large circular bowl with a square pillar rising from its center placed on a square pedestal. The main bowl was intended for horses to water and was fed by bronze spigots in the shape of lion heads on three sides. The fourth side contained a bronze plaque listing the donors' names and the date of the donation. The lower pedestal had niches on each side with drinking bowls near ground level for dogs, cats and other small animals.

In 1919, an unfortunate event occurred at the Cheyenne location. According to news reports, a horse-drawn wagon crashed into the fountain after the horses were startled by a fire truck. One passenger in the wagon was thrown out, and another passenger clung to the wagon as the horses hurtled toward the fountain. As the animals struggled to get around the fountain, the wagon hit it and knocked off the top of the structure. News accounts reported that it was good luck that no one was killed.

A few years later, the fountain was moved to another location in Cheyenne where it was no longer hooked to a water supply. According to Steve Vandehei, his grandfather Earl Vandehei obtained the fountain after he discovered it was about to be demolished. Earl paid a crew $250 to move the structure to his ranch north of Cheyenne. He was fond of the fountain because he used to ride his horse from his ranch to Cheyenne and water the animal at the fountain near the Union Pacific Depot.

Left: The Humane Alliance Fountain once stood at the intersection of Carey Avenue and 15th Street, providing a place for horses and other animals to find a drink of water. *J.E. Stimson Collection, Wyoming State Archives, Department of State Parks and Cultural Resources.*

Below: A portion of the Humane Alliance Fountain was moved to Lakeview Cemetery at the final resting place of Earl Vandehei, a rancher who used to ride his horse to Cheyenne and water the animal at the fountain. *Starley Talbott photograph.*

After Earl died, his son, Jerry Vandehei, and son-in-law, Tom Kilty, had a portion of the fountain moved to his gravesite at Lakeview Cemetery. The block that was originally above the bowl and included the lion head faucets is at the home of another family member (minus the lion head faucets). The portion above the bowl at the cemetery is not from the original fountain. It was purchased and engraved with the names Vandehei and Kilty. Earl Vandehei's monument serves as a fitting memorial because it provided Earl's horses with water and a rest after their long journey, and now it serves to mark his final resting place.

Chapter 4

STROLLING AND MOTORING AROUND CHEYENNE

The Cheyenne downtown historic district is very walkable. While there are many roads with the name of *Avenue*, the principal north–south avenues within the downtown corridor are Thomes Avenue, Pioneer Avenue, Carey Avenue, Capitol Avenue, Central Avenue, Warren Avenue, House Avenue and Evans Avenue. The streets within the walkable downtown district are 26th Street on the north end and 15th Street on the south end. (This is not an official designation of the historic district but one the authors determined to be a walkable area.)

Several Cheyenne entities have established walking and trolley tours of the historic downtown area. Many of the buildings, monuments and murals have been more thoroughly discussed in previous chapters of this book. Readers are encouraged to visit the Cheyenne Depot Museum and inquire about the historic Trolley Tour and other Cheyenne events.

The Cheyenne Street Railway Trolley offers Wild West narrated tours from May through September, departing from the Historic Railroad Depot and the Cheyenne Botanic Gardens. Specialty tours include the Ghost Frightseeing Tours in October and Holiday Light Tours in December.

Scattered throughout Cheyenne are more than thirty hand-painted eight-foot-tall cowpoke boots designed to tell stories of historic events in the city. When strolling or motoring the avenues and streets of the city, look for these boots that are artistic monuments dedicated to Cheyenne's past and present.

"These Boots Are Made for Talking" began as a joint project of the Cheyenne Depot Museum Foundation and the Downtown Development

Left: Cowpoke boots, standing eight feet tall and decorated by local artists, are on display throughout Cheyenne, telling stories of the past and present. *Starley Talbott photograph.*

Below: The Cheyenne Street Railway Trolley provides narrated tours of historic Cheyenne during the summer season and at other holiday times. *Starley Talbott photograph.*

Authority. Each boot was painted by one or more area artists with the theme "If this boot could talk, what story would it tell?" Boots have been added to the collection each year. Many boots can be discovered when exploring the historic downtown district. There are several of the boot statues on the Depot Plaza. More information can be obtained at the Historic Depot.

After visiting the historic downtown, there are many other areas of Cheyenne with historical significance. Earlier chapters explore many of these places. While no book can cover everything about a city, an attempt has been made to include many important historical aspects of Cheyenne. The authors apologize if your favorite place has not been included. We hope you will explore the roots of Cheyenne and then spread your wings to learn more about our fascinating city.

BIBLIOGRAPHY

Adams, Gerald M. "The Air Age Comes to Wyoming." *Annals of Wyoming* 52, no. 2 (1980).

———. *The Post Near Cheyenne: A History of Fort D.A. Russell, 1867–1930*. Boulder, CO: Pruett Publishing Company, 1989.

Airport Improvement. "Cheyenne Area's New Terminal Poised to Meet Region's Air Service Needs." January–February 2019. airportimprovement.com/article/cheyenne-area-s-new-terminal-poised-meet-region-s-air-service-needs.

Amundson, Michael A. *Wyoming Revisited: Rephotographing the Scenes of Joseph E. Stimson*. Boulder: University Press of Colorado, 2014.

Arnold, Bess, and James L. Ehernberger. *Union Pacific Depot: An Elegant Legacy to Cheyenne*. Cheyenne, WY: Challenger Press, 2001.

Austin, Margaret, and Tom Coulter. "F.E. Warren Nuclear Missiles to Be Replaced First, Creating More Than 1,000 Jobs." *Wyoming Tribune Eagle*, August 14, 2020.

Black, Robert W. "Farewell to the Peacekeeper: F.E. Warren Continues to Operate 150 Minuteman III Missiles." *Casper Star Tribune*, September 20, 2005.

Carlson, Chip. "Tom Horn: Wyoming Enigma." WyoHistory.org: A Project of the Wyoming State Historical Society. November 8, 2014. www.wyohistory.org.

Cheyenne Centennial Committee. *The Magic City of the Plains: Cheyenne 1867–1967*. Cheyenne, WY, 1967.

Cheyenne Daily Leader. "Ensign Fountain Dedicated Yesterday." May 23, 1908.

Cook, Malcolm L. *First Church: A People Called Methodist*. Cheyenne, WY: First United Methodist Church, 1993.

Cummings, Kathryn Swim. *Esther Hobart Morris*. Glendo, WY: High Plains Press, 2019.

Davis, Monica Asher. Interview with author Talbott, June 2, 2021.

Dixon, Michael. *Cheyenne Wyoming Downtown Tour*. Brochure, 2019.

Ewig, Rick. *Cheyenne: A Sesquicentennial History*. San Antonio, TX: HPN Books, 2017.

———. "The Letters of John A. Feick." *Annals of Wyoming* 59, no. 1 (Spring 1987): 2–14.

Ewig, Rick, Linda Rollins and Betty Griffin. *Wyoming's Capitol*. Cheyenne: Wyoming State Press, 1987.

Feick, John Adam, and Feick Brothers. Letters. Wyoming State Archives.

Feinberg, John D., and Ellen T. Ittelson. *Cheyenne's Historic Architecture*. Prepared for the Cheyenne–Laramie County Regional Planning Office. Cheyenne, WY.

Field, Sharon Lass, ed. *History of Cheyenne, Wyoming: Laramie County*. Vol. 2. N.p.: Curtis Media Corporation, 1989, 38, 64–72, 75–79, 105–16, 165, 174, 486.

Fike, Ellen. "F.E. Warren Unveils Air Park." *Wyoming Tribune Eagle*, June 11, 2021.

Flynn, Shirley. *Let's Go! Let's Show! Let's Rodeo! The History of Cheyenne Frontier Days*. Cheyenne, WY: Wigwam Publishing Company, LLC, 1996.

Fraser, Clayton B. "Cheyenne Airfield, Fountain (HAER WY-83-B)." *Historic American Engineering Record*, 2009.

Girt, Rachel. "Jelineks Create Vibrant Gathering Spaces in Downtown." *Wyoming Tribune Eagle*, Our Faces, March 2021.

———. "Saving Wyoming's Architectural Treasure for Future Generations." *Wyoming Rural Electric News*, July 2017.

Hanesworth, Robert D. *Daddy of 'Em All: The Story of Cheyenne Frontier Days*. Cheyenne, WY: Flintlock Publishing Company, 1967.

Hoffman, Megan. "Wyoming Army National Guard Receives Aviation Additions." dvidshub.net/news/printable/194547.

Holmes, Beverly. "The Wyoming National Guard Museum: Cheyenne, Wyoming 2007 to Present." E-mail document received by author Kassel from William Saunders, April 28, 2021.

Humstone, Mary M. "Cheyenne Airport Old Terminal Building and Fountain." SAH Archipedia. sah-archipedia.org/buildings/WY-01-021-0009.

Kassel, Michael E. "Thunder on High: Cheyenne, Denver and Aviation Supremacy on the Rocky Mountain Front Range." Master's thesis, University of Wyoming, 2007.

———. "The United Airlines Stewardess School in Cheyenne." *Annals of Wyoming* 75, no. 4 (Autumn 2003): 11–18.

Klein, Maury. *Union Pacific*. Vol. 1, *1862–1893*. Minneapolis: University of Minnesota Press, 1987.

Laramie County Chapter, Wyoming State Historical Society. *Cheyenne Landmarks*. Cheyenne, WY: Pioneer Printing, 1976.

Larson, T.A. *History of Wyoming*. Lincoln: University of Nebraska Press, 1963.

Lightner, Sam, Jr. *Wyoming: A History of the American West*. N.p.: 2020.

Mercado, Irving. "Brief History of LCCC Athletics." *Wingspan Magazine*, September 30, 2018.

Moulton, Candy. *Roadside History of Wyoming*. Missoula, MT: Mountain Press Publishing Company, 1995.

Moulton, Candy, and Flossie Moulton. *Steamboat*. Glendo, WY: High Plains Press, 1992.

Newman, Deidre. E-mail communications with author Talbott, May 25–28, 2021.

O'Neal, Bill. *Cheyenne: A Biography of the "Magic City" of the Plains*. Austin, TX: Eakin Press, 2006.

Page, Ashley, and the Cheyenne Depot Museum. *The Cheyenne Depot*. Charleston, SC: Arcadia Publishing, 2020.

Plambeck, Maurice. "Boeing/United Airlines Terminal Building, Hangar and Fountain." Laramie County, Wyoming. National Register of Historic Places Inventory, Registration Form, 1983. National Park Service, U.S. Department of the Interior, Washington, D.C.

Rea, Tom. "Buffalo Soldiers in Wyoming and the West." WyoHistory.org: A Project of the Wyoming State Historical Society. January 30, 2015.

Riske, Milt. *Cheyenne Frontier Days: A Marker from Which to Reckon All Events*. Cheyenne, WY: Frontier Printing, Inc., 1984.

Rosenberg, Robert G. "Cheyenne Airfield." Historic American Engineering Record, Denver, CO, 1998.

———. "Cheyenne Airport Property Building and Structures Inventory." Wyoming Historic Architecture Inventory Form, Cheyenne, WY, 1997.

Soule, David. "Expanding New Horizons: Albany Campus Expansion." *Wingspan Magazine*, February 15, 2019.

Talbott, Starley, and Linda Graves Fabian. *Cheyenne Frontier Days*. Charleston, SC: Arcadia Publishing, 2013.

———. *A History of the Wyoming Capitol*. Charleston, SC: The History Press, 2019.

Talbott, Starley, and Michael E. Kassel. *Wyoming Airmail Pioneers*. Charleston, SC: The History Press, 2017.

———. *Wyoming's Friendly Skies*. Charleston, SC: The History Press, 2020.

Talon Magazine. Vol. 26 (Summer 2018). lccc.wy.edu/about/publicRelations/talon-magazine/2018-summer-vol-26/nationallyRecognized.aspx.

Taylor, Paula Bauman. *F.E. Warren Air Force Base*. Charleston, SC: Arcadia Publishing, 2012.

Vandehei, Steve. E-mail communications with author Talbott, May 13–20, 2021.

Van Pelt, Lori. *Capital Characters of Old Cheyenne*. Glendo, WY: High Plains Press, 2006.

———. "Cheyenne, Magic City of the Plains." WyoHistory.org: A Project of the Wyoming State Historical Society. October 30, 2017.

Weidel, Nancy. *Cheyenne: 1867–1917*. Charleston, SC: Arcadia Publishing, 2009.

Wolff, A.J., and J.L. Ehernberger. *Union Pacific's Cheyenne Facilities*. Halifax, PA: Withers Publishing, 2020.

Wyoming Air National Guard. "History." www.153aw.ang.af.mil/Resources/History.

Wyoming Army National Guard Historic Buildings Field Inventory and Evaluation Report. University of Wyoming American Studies Program, June 2007.

Wyoming Eagle. "Boeing Enlarges Building Program Here." August 23, 1929.

Wyoming Military Department. "Heritage and History." www.wyomilitary.wyo.gov/guard/history.

Wyoming State Tribune. "Theater Was Institution Here." April 27, 1981.

WEBSITES

Cheyenne Botanic Gardens. www.botanic.org.

Cheyenne Frontier Days Old West Museum. www.oldwestmuseum.org.

Cheyenne Street Railway Trolley. www.cheyennetrolley.com.

Cowgirls of the West. www.cowgirlsofthewestmuseum.com.

Laramie County Community College. www.lccc.wy.edu.

Military Memorial Museum. militarymemorialmuseum.org.

Nelson Museum of the West. nelsonmuseum.org.

Visit Cheyenne. www.cheyenne.org.
WyoHistory.org: A Project of the Wyoming State Historical Society. wyohistory.org.
Wyoming National Guard Museum. www.wyngm.wyo.gov.
Wyoming Newspapers: From the Wyoming State Library. newspapers.wyo.gov.
Wyoming State Archives. wyoarchives.state.wyo.us.
Wyoming State Historic Preservation Office. wyoshpo.state.wyo.us.

ABOUT THE AUTHORS

Starley Talbott has been a freelance author for more than forty years. She has been published in numerous newspapers and magazines throughout the Rocky Mountain region and is the author of nine books, including three Arcadia Publishing titles: *Platte County*, *Fort Laramie* and *Cheyenne Frontier Days*; and three History Press titles: *Wyoming Airmail Pioneers*, *A History of the Wyoming Capitol* and *Wyoming's Friendly Skies*. Starley holds a BS degree from the University of Wyoming and an MS degree from the University of Nevada. She has lived in several states and foreign countries, loves to travel and has a deep appreciation for history. She is a member of Wyoming Writers, Platte County Historical Society and the Wyoming State Historical Society.

Michael E. Kassel serves as the curator of collections and the associate director of operations at the Cheyenne Frontier Days™ Old West Museum. He is an adjunct professor of history at Laramie County Community College in Cheyenne, Wyoming. He holds a BS degree in historic preservation from Southeast Missouri State University, an associate of the arts degree in history from Laramie County Community College and a master of arts degree from the University of Wyoming. He is the author of *Thunder on High: Cheyenne, Denver and Aviation Supremacy on the Rocky Mountain Front Range* and *The United Air Lines Stewardess School in Cheyenne, Wyoming*. He is the co-author of *Wyoming Airmail Pioneers* and *Wyoming's Friendly Skies* from The History Press.